The Virtue of Open-Mindedness and Perspective

THE VIRTUES: MULTIDISCIPLINARY PERSPECTIVES

Series Editor

Nancy E. Snow
Professor of Philosophy, University of Kansas

Justice
Edited by Mark LeBar

Humility
Edited by Jennifer Cole Wright

Integrity, Honesty, and Truth- Seeking
Edited by Christian B. Miller and Ryan West

The Virtues of Sustainability
Edited by Jason Kawall

The Virtue of Harmony
Edited by Chenyang Li and Dascha Düring

The Virtue of Loyalty
Edited by Troy Jollimore

The Virtue of Solidarity
Edited by Andrea Sangiovanni and Juri Viehoff

The Virtue of Hope
Edited by Nancy E. Snow

The Virtues of Endurance
Edited by Nathan L. King

The Virtue of Open-Mindedness and Perspective
Edited by Wayne D. Riggs

The Virtue of Open-Mindedness and Perspective

Edited by
WAYNE D. RIGGS

OXFORD
UNIVERSITY PRESS

Oxford University Press is a department of the University of Oxford.
It furthers the University's objective of excellence in research, scholarship,
and education by publishing worldwide. Oxford is a registered trade mark of
Oxford University Press in the UK and in certain other countries.

Published in the United States of America by Oxford University Press
198 Madison Avenue, New York, NY 10016, United States of America.

© Oxford University Press 2025

All rights reserved. No part of this publication may be reproduced, stored in a retrieval system, transmitted, used for text and data mining, or used for training artificial intelligence, in any form or by any means, without the prior permission in writing of Oxford University Press, or as expressly permitted by law, by license or under terms agreed with the appropriate reprographics rights organization. Inquiries concerning reproduction outside the scope of the above should be sent to the Rights Department, Oxford University Press, at the address above.

You must not circulate this work in any other form
and you must impose this same condition on any acquirer.

Library of Congress Cataloging-in-Publication Data
Names: Riggs, Wayne D., editor.
Title: The virtue of open-mindedness and perspective / edited by Wayne D. Riggs.
Description: 1. | New York, NY : Oxford University Press, [2025] |
Series: The virtues : multidisciplinary perspectives |
Includes bibliographical references and index.
Identifiers: LCCN 2025002307 (print) | LCCN 2025002308 (ebook) |
ISBN 9780190080693 (paperback) | ISBN 9780190080686 (hardback) |
ISBN 9780190080723 | ISBN 9780190080716 (epub)
Subjects: LCSH: Fairness. | Perspective (Philosophy)
Classification: LCC BJ1533.F2 V56 2025 (print) | LCC BJ1533.F2 (ebook) |
DDC 179/.9—dc23/eng/20250215
LC record available at https://lccn.loc.gov/2025002307
LC ebook record available at https://lccn.loc.gov/2025002308

DOI: 10.1093/9780190080723.001.0001

Paperback printed by Marquis Book Printing, Canada
Hardback printed by Bridgeport National Bindery, Inc., United States of America

Contents

Series Editor's Foreword	vii
Contributor Biographies	ix
Introduction	1
Wayne D. Riggs	
1. Perspectival Complacency, Perversion, and Amelioration	19
Elisabeth Camp	
2. Perspective-Taking and a Flexible Mind: A Tibetan Buddhist Approach to Open-Mindedness	58
Emily McRae	
3. A Trickster's Sideways Look at Open-Mindedness as a Virtue: A Native American Perspective	79
Rockey Robbins and Howard Bad Hand	
4. Free Speech and Challenges to Open-Mindedness in Higher Education	101
Emily Robertson	
5. Jacques Copeau's Theater and Masks: Actor Training as Formation in Open-Mindedness	122
Margaret (Peggy) Garvey	
6. How to Be Open-Minded: Ask Good Questions (and Listen to the Answers)	139
Lani Watson	
Index	169

Series Editor's Foreword

Typically, having a virtue means being disposed to having certain kinds of perceptions, thoughts, motives, emotions, and ways one is inclined to act. The end of the twentieth and the beginning of the twenty-first centuries have seen an upsurge of interest in the topic of virtue. This is true not only in philosophy but also in a variety of other disciplines, such as theology, law, economics, psychology, and anthropology, to name a few. The study of virtue within disciplines is vitally important, yet the premise of this series is that the study of virtue in general, as well as of specific virtues, can be enhanced if scholars take into account work being done in disciplines other than their own.

Cross-disciplinary work can be challenging. Scholars trained in one field with its unique vocabulary and methods do not always move seamlessly into another discipline and often feel unqualified to undertake the task of serious cross-disciplinary engagement. The upshot can be that practitioners of disciplines can become "siloed"— trapped within their own disciplines and hesitant to engage seriously with others, even on important topics of mutual interest.

This series seeks to break the silos, with fifteen volumes on specific virtues or clusters of virtues. For each book, an introduction by the editor highlights the unity of writings by identifying common themes, threads, and ideas. In each volume, the editor seeks to include a chapter from a "wild card" discipline, a field one would not expect to see included in a collection of essays on a particular virtue. We do this both to highlight the diversity of fields in the study of specific virtues and to surprise and challenge readers to broaden their horizons in thinking about virtue.

The audience for this series is practitioners of different disciplines who seek to expand their thinking about virtue. Each volume contains chapters that are accessible and of interest to scholars from many disciplines. Though the volumes are not comprehensive overviews of the work on virtue that is occurring in any given field, they provide a

viii   SERIES EDITOR'S FOREWORD

useful introduction meant to pique the curiosity of readers and spur further engagement with other disciplines.

Nancy E. Snow
Professor of Philosophy
University of Kansas

Contributor Biographies

Howard Bad Hand is a Sicangu Lakota from Rosebud, South Dakota, and was educated at the Lenox School, Dartmouth College, Harvard University, and Sinte Gleska College. A fourth-generation member of a family of singers known as song keepers for the Sicangu Lakota, he is a singer and composer of Lakota songs. He is intercessor of High Star Sun Eagle sun dance. Howard lives in Taos, New Mexico, with his wife, Terry.

Elisabeth Camp is professor of philosophy at Rutgers. She obtained her PhD from the University of California, Berkeley, held a post-doc at the Harvard Society of Fellows, and taught at the University of Pennsylvania before moving to Rutgers in 2013. She is the author of more than thirty articles in the philosophy of language, mind, and aesthetics. Her work focuses on thoughts and utterances that don't fit a standard propositionalist model of minds and languages, including metaphor, maps, and animal cognition. Recent publications include an edited volume, *The Poetry of Emily Dickinson: Philosophical Perspectives* (Oxford University Press, 2021); "Language: Power Plays at the Edges of Communication," in *Philosophy for Girls: An Invitation to the Life of Thought* (Oxford University Press, 2020); and "Imaginative Frames for Scientific Inquiry: Metaphors, Telling Facts, and Just-So Stories" (in *The Scientific Imagination,* Oxford University Press, 2019).

Margaret (Peggy) Garvey, PhD, is currently executive director of the Elms University Center and associate artistic director of the Athenaeum Center for Thought and Culture in Chicago. An educator for over thirty years, she holds degrees in Classics, theater arts, and literature. Her interdisciplinary dissertation focused on the educational philosophy of the revolutionary theater director Jacques Copeau. She has a passionate interest in theater art's educational essence and its unique power to form actors, theater-makers, and audiences. While at the University of Notre Dame, she collaborated with academics from all over the world at the interdisciplinary Notre Dame Institute for Advanced Study and organized an international conference, "The Actor as Person." She has directed plays as varied as *Exit the King* and *Riders to the Sea*. Most recently, she co-directed *Dante 360* at the Athenaeum in Chicago and is currently co-directing a one-man performance of T. S. Eliot's *Four Quartets*.

X CONTRIBUTOR BIOGRAPHIES

Emily McRae is an associate professor of philosophy at the University of New Mexico. She specializes in Tibetan Buddhist philosophy, ethics, moral psychology, and feminism. Much of her work is in the philosophy of emotions and the philosophy of interpersonal relationships. She has published articles on these topics in *American Philosophical Quarterly*, *Philosophy East and West*, *Journal of Religious Ethics*, and *History of Philosophy Quarterly*. With the support of the National Endowment for the Humanities Award for Faculty, she is currently writing a book on Indo-Tibetan philosophical approaches to moral ignorance.

Wayne D. Riggs is professor of philosophy at the University of Oklahoma. His primary interest is epistemology, and he has published on topics in virtue epistemology (including open-mindedness in particular) as well as on epistemic luck, epistemic values, and the theory of knowledge.

Rockey Robbins, PhD (Choctaw/Cherokee), served as a professor in counseling psychology at the University of Oklahoma for twenty-three years before his retirement in 2022. His research focuses primarily on the relationship between Native American spirituality and Western psychology. He has published dozens of scientific articles in his field. He has also conducted workshops and given speeches on these topics to both specialists and public audiences around the world. He has been instrumental in encouraging the application of philosophical concepts to psychological theorizing and treatment.

Emily Robertson is professor emerita from Syracuse University, where she was a member of the Cultural Foundations of Education Department, School of Education, and the Philosophy Department, College of Arts and Sciences. She is a philosopher of education whose work focuses on epistemology and education, the development of rationality as an educational ideal, and democratic education. Robertson was interim dean and associate dean of the School of Education at Syracuse. She is a past president of the Philosophy of Education Society. In 2017 she published (with Jon Zimmerman) *The Case for Contention: Teaching Controversial Issues in American Schools* (Chicago University Press). Recent articles include her AESA Kneller lecture, "Testimonial Virtue" (*Educational Studies*) and "The Epistemic Value of Diversity" (*Journal of Philosophy of Education*).

Lani Watson is a research fellow at the University of Oxford. Her research focuses on questions and questioning and she works primarily in contemporary epistemology, including in virtue, social and political epistemology, and the epistemology of education. She has published multiple papers highlighting the value and significance of questioning, both within academic philosophy and in public and professional settings. Her work is continually expanding to encompass the use of questions in professional practice in organizational contexts ranging from health care institutions to military intelligence; across classrooms, courtrooms, and boardrooms; and in public debate and media discourse. She is currently writing a book for a wide public audience on the topic of questions, due for publication with the Bodley Head, Penguin, in 2025. Her first book on the topic of epistemic rights was published in 2021 with Routledge, titled *The Right to Know: Epistemic Rights and Why We Need Them.*

Introduction

Wayne D. Riggs

This volume considers open-mindedness primarily as an epistemic virtue. It seems fairly clear that there are corresponding virtues of open-mindedness that are moral and perhaps civic as well, and there are likely not sharp boundaries between. But here we shall consider open-mindedness primarily in its epistemic guise.

Though philosopher-heavy, this volume has contributions from a variety of fields. The resulting multi-focal discourse is not so much a sustained deep dive into the nature of some agreed-upon pre-theoretical notion of open-mindedness (though there is certainly some discussion of that) but rather a broad investigation into the various ways consideration of things like educational structures, contemplative practices, cognitive and conceptual architecture, popular culture, colonialization, good questioning practices, and training in the arts can help define the boundaries and provide the details of a rich and adequate conception of open-mindedness.

The first part of this essay will describe an approach to theorizing in epistemology and, hence, to the narrower project of theorizing about open-mindedness as an epistemic virtue. This approach, to my mind, frames (in a specifically epistemological light) the subsequent essays in this volume and highlights some of what I take to be their central contributions. I am in no way attributing the details of this philosophical approach to any of the contributors, who may disagree with any or all of what I have to say. Each of their essays should, of course, be taken and understood on its own terms. Subsequently, I will discuss some common themes throughout the chapters in this volume, providing a brief summary of each one.

Wayne D. Riggs, *Introduction* In: *The Virtue of Open-Mindedness and Perspective.*
Edited by: Wayne D. Riggs, Oxford University Press. © Oxford University Press 2025.
DOI: 10.1093/9780190080723.003.0001

2 THE VIRTUE OF OPEN-MINDEDNESS

1 Naturalism in Epistemology

Normative theorizing in philosophy faces a general problem. We typically want our normative theories to be obviously applicable to the creatures whom we are interested in theorizing about—typically human beings. This imposes a constraint on those theories to take sufficiently into account the contingent nature of human beings, at least insofar as it is relevant to the particular normative notion being characterized. This means that our theorizing must descend somewhat from the Platonic heavens to pay at least some attention to the various accounts of those contingent features of humanity provided by the various branches of the sciences.

Yet this movement toward psychological, sociological, neurological, anthropological, etc. realism in our philosophical theories has a cost. The very normativity we set out intending to capture can seem to elude us once we move from abstract, conceptual characterizations of the phenomena in question to detailed, descriptive accounts of how embodied humans in particular physical and social environments actually function. We want to be able to offer criteria to determine when one has made substantive connection with "the Good," whether that be in moral, aesthetic, or epistemic terms. But once we are talking about the specific contingencies of actual human performance, it is hard to see where the resources for constructing such a normative standard would come from.

This problem arises for epistemology as much as it does for any other so-called normative domain in philosophy. Matt Chrisman has a nice discussion of this in the Introduction to his book *Belief, Agency, and Knowledge*. Chrisman articulates two desiderata of epistemological theorizing that he would like to achieve in his own work. First, the preservation of epistemology as a deeply normative discipline. He wants to address questions like "Why do we prize knowledge over true belief? Do the rules of theoretical rationality have categorically binding normative force? . . . What are the intellectual virtues?"[1] Second, a commitment to a version of naturalism, specifically a commitment to the generally accepted idea that beliefs are, in some important sense, involuntary. He sums up the puzzle he poses himself like this: "If knowledge ascriptions entail that someone believes as they normatively ought to believe . . . then believing must normally be within the scope of our immediate agency; but involuntarism and naturalism commit us to the idea that our agency touches our beliefs only atypically and indirectly."[2] The details of Chrisman's project need not detain us; the point is that Chrisman urges a commitment to these forms of naturalism but also highlights the challenge that poses to someone like himself who wants to account for the rich normativity that seems inherent in epistemology.

The study of epistemic virtues (like open-mindedness) has to navigate this same terrain. Indeed, it's situation is, if anything, more acute, since historically the idea of a virtue came from a prior theory of human nature. Virtues are, for Aristotle, excellences in the way of being paradigmatically human. If we are to be naturalists in the manner of Chrisman, we need to provide a theory of open-mindedness that is true to what the natural sciences have to teach us about human beings, particularly about the operation of our minds. The resulting picture is very different from that with which epistemology has proceeded for most of its history, though consonant with a picture that is emerging in very recent work from a variety of sub-fields of philosophy.[3]

Among the things the natural and social sciences have taught us about ourselves is that we are not the generic, abstract, isolated, self-sufficient, atomistic agents assumed by, for example, a classically Cartesian theoretical framework. More precisely, we have learned that our actual cognitive proceedings work in ways so different from what those idealizing assumptions allow that those assumptions are not always helpful for theorizing about human cognizers. The theoretical parameters set by such a conception of cognitive agents is neither empirically nor normatively adequate. The descriptive content seems just empirically false and, consequently, the normative demands seem impossible for actual humans to meet.[4]

So precisely how should all this revelatory scientific work inform our epistemological theorizing? That is too big a question to address here. However, I will, perhaps surprisingly, take a cue from Descartes. One reason that Descartes's arguments are so compelling is that he grounds them in a conception of what I will call the human epistemological predicament (HEP). He articulates a vivid picture of our cognitive powers and limitations and the epistemic goals we hope to

4 THE VIRTUE OF OPEN-MINDEDNESS

achieve by way of them. The particular way he conceived of the predicament channels the possible solutions down some paths and not others. In the next section, I will take a brief look at the HEP assumed and described by Descartes and then propose an updated version that might guide and inform our theorizing about open-mindedness.

2 The Human Epistemological Predicament

Our epistemological theories reflect our conception of the (HEP). A predicament, as commonly understood, inherently involves a set of problems or difficulties, along with the resources available to address the problems or difficulties. To get a handle on what this means, let's consider the predicament implicit in Descartes's epistemology. The fundamental problem, for Descartes, was how to achieve certainty in our beliefs. It's a problem because we desire such certainty but in the ordinary course of events, we form beliefs in such a way that they are not, in fact, certain. The only resources available to us to address this problem, according to Descartes, are those within each of our individual minds. In other words, this is not a collective problem for us to solve but a problem each of us has to solve using only the contents of our individual consciousnesses.

Though Descartes's conception of the HEP has been very influential throughout the subsequent history of epistemology, most aspects of it no longer resonate with contemporary philosophers. This suggests the need for a new understanding of our HEP to help clarify the epistemological landscape and guide theorizing. There are a few features of this new understanding that are particularly salient to our concerns here.

First, few epistemologists still think the appropriate epistemic goal is certainty. Most would settle for a decent shot at true belief—or, perhaps, another epistemic good like understanding, wisdom, justified belief, knowledge, epistemic virtue, etc. Or perhaps even, as will become more pertinent below, discernment in judging good sources of information from a confusing and sometimes deceptive social environment.

Second, the kinds of obstacles to certainty that Descartes is worried about are generic and abstract—e.g., the inherent unreliability of sense perception and the bare possibility of being deceived about virtually anything we believe. This highlights what has been described as the "atomism"[5] inherent in this approach. The problems encountered are problems that any generic epistemic agent encounters. Specific, unique, or idiosyncratic features of the individual, her circumstances, social position, etc. are not relevant to the problem to be solved.

Third, and relatedly, the conception is almost hyperbolically individualist. The problem of finding a ground for certainty for our beliefs can (only) be addressed by each of us alone. Moreover, it is our own special and unique responsibility to do so. The failure to purge the mind of falsehoods is one for which we, as agents, are (solely) responsible. Descartes hoped to help others achieve it, but only by describing the method that each person must individually pursue.

It is now widely acknowledged that when someone does find epistemic success, it is rarely through the workings of their individual mind alone. We are social creatures through and through. The human way of living in the world is to meet our fundamental needs by banding together. It's been a long time, evolutionarily speaking, since humans (or our progenitors) were able to thrive by meeting their needs independently of other conspecifics. We feed, clothe, and shelter ourselves collectively. Similarly, it's been a very long time, evolutionarily speaking, since humans were able to meet our cognitive needs independently of other human beings. We think collectively as well.

This can be understood more or less radically, and this is not a battle to be fought here. It is enough to acknowledge what is clear enough, which is that as fully formed cognitive adults we at least still rely heavily on the testimony of others. And as developing cognitive agents we rely on parents, teachers, mentors, educators, etc. to help us become fully formed cognitive adults. Moving slightly farther down the road of socialized epistemology, it is now hard to deny that epistemic goods of all kinds can be "distributed" inequitably. The material circumstances under which it is possible to gain access to epistemic goods, the social conditions under which one can be acknowledged as a possessor and legitimate purveyor of epistemic goods, the psychological and social support needed to fully develop into an integrated, autonomous epistemic agent—these are all things that can be inequitably distributed and the results will have epistemic consequences for individuals and

6   THE VIRTUE OF OPEN-MINDEDNESS

epistemic communities alike. It takes a village for any individual to (eventually) achieve epistemic success.

Finally, Descartes was famously a dualist, and drew a very sharp distinction between mind and body. It was with the mind, through our divinely wrought "natural light of reason," that we were able to "see" clearly and distinctly enough to achieve certainty. Proper use of such a lofty faculty would save us from epistemological failure. And this faculty was wholly (ontologically, at least) independent of our physical body. More to the present point, the embodiment of our minds played no significant role in its proper operation and in no significant way contributed to our achievement of the epistemic goal—certainty in our beliefs.

Now we know, contra Descartes, our cognitive functioning depends crucially on the bodies we inhabit. The negative aspects of this have received a lot of attention. For instance, it is well-known that humans are prone to all sorts of biases, prejudices, and motivated reasoning that are a function of our brain's evolutionary past. And in general, much of what we think is the product of so-called system 1 processes whose provenance is completely opaque to us, and whose reliability at getting us to the truth is often suspect (or at least highly contextual and contingent). Importantly, these are not simply the result of sloppy thinking or careless disregard of our cognitive duties; rather, in general, they are instances of the way that evolution molded our cognitive processes. It is unclear precisely what degree of control we have over these aspects of our cognitive lives, but it is clear that such control as we have is nowhere near total.[6] Hence, no matter what we do, we are going to be subject to the influence of these processes to some extent.

There are positive aspects to this cognitive architecture as well, of course. Heuristics are fast, biases are efficient, etc. And whether we see them as good or bad can depend on what resources we take ourselves to have to train them up properly and/or correct them when they go astray. Such resources may be different from the kinds of things that epistemologists have traditionally focused on.

In their book, book *The Enigma of Reason*,[7] Mercier and Sperber do a nice job motivating, articulating, and defending something like the updated HEP I am sketching here. According to these two authors, it is hard to reconcile two apparent facts. The first is that human powers of reasoning are considered to be a kind of "superpower" among evolved cognitive traits:

> We are told that reason . . . is a general-purpose faculty. Reason elevates cognition to new heights. Without reason, animal cognition is bound by instinct; knowledge and action are dramatically limited. Enhanced with reason, cognition can secure better knowledge in all domains and adjust action to novel and ambitious goals.[8]

The second is that humans are apparently really bad at reasoning:

> Psychologists claim to have shown that human reason is flawed. The idea that reason does its job quite poorly has become commonplace. Experiment after experiment has convinced psychologists and philosophers that people make egregious mistakes in reasoning. And it is not just that people reason poorly, it is that they are systematically biased.[9]

Humans have clearly managed astounding epistemic achievements. How can this be if the capacities we have for doing so are so systematically flawed? Mercier and Sperber spend the rest of their book making the case for their answer to this question, which is, roughly, that the practice of dredging up and consciously considering reasons for our beliefs and actions did not evolve primarily to make us better at arriving at truths individually. It evolved to allow us to justify our already held commitments to beliefs and actions, both to ourselves and to others. Individual reasoning is, as the literature has shown time and again, biased and lazy. Left to ourselves, we are not likely to succeed epistemically. But, as the authors argue, this is not the purpose of reasoning.

> What, then, happens when reason is put back in its "normal" environment, when it gets to work in the midst of a discussion, as people exchange arguments and justifications with each other? In such a context it properly fulfills the functions for which it evolved. In particular, when people who disagree but have a common interest in finding the truth or the solution to a problem exchange arguments

8 THE VIRTUE OF OPEN-MINDEDNESS

> with one another, the best idea tends to win.... This conclusion may
> sound unduly optimistic, but it is supported by a wide range of evi-
> dence. (p. 10)[10]

Sloman and Fernbach come to a similar conclusion in their book, *The Knowledge Illusion*.[11]

> These examples illustrate one of the key properties of the
> mind: It did not evolve in the context of individuals sitting alone
> solving problems. It evolved in the context of group collaboration,
> and our thinking evolved interdependently, to operate in conjunc-
> tion with the thinking of others.[12]

If the general idea behind these theories is right, an exclusive focus on the individual in our epistemology is never going to be "naturalistic" in the sense discussed above. Our epistemic predicament is one in which we are, as a matter of practical, evolved necessity, dependent on other humans to succeed epistemically. Hence, our theories that purport to describe epistemic goods toward which we aspire must take this inter-dependence into account.

To sum up this brief reflection, we humans are embodied and so-cial creatures who make our epistemic way in the world by relying crucially on bodily processes, embedded information in the world, ep-istemic communities, and the kindness of strangers. This comparative modesty about our epistemic powers suggests an attendant modesty in our epistemic aims. Finding a proposition about which we are incor-rigible might no longer seem like the most pressing epistemological issue. How can I minimize the influences of confirmation bias, per-nicious stereotypes, and perspectival limitations on my thinking and consequent beliefs? Can I be said to have genuine knowledge if what I believe is based on what someone else told me? How do I know if I'm stuck in an echo chamber, and what can I do about it if I am? Given my deep epistemic dependence on others, can I be said to know anything at all? If so, how? These questions come to the fore on this new concep-tion of the human epistemological predicament. As it happens, many of these are questions that a theory of open-mindedness is well-placed to begin to answer.

3 Open-Mindedness

It is interesting just how central open-mindedness starts to look once we begin taking the new HEP seriously. On this new picture, for example, it seems clear that we will often get "stuck" in a way of thinking because of the influence of bias produced by deep, un-introspectable cognitive processes. Since we know we are prone to these influences, and we know they can lead us astray from the truth, there is a premium on finding ways to counter their influence on us. That seems an excellent motivation for a theory of open-mindedness. On the other hand, it also poses a direct challenge to such theories. The influences of these deep biases are notoriously hard to overcome. Not only do these considerations indicate a need for a theory of open-mindedness, but they also point to considerations an adequate theory should address itself to. If being open-minded doesn't help with combating deep psychological bias, then it is less useful than it might be in helping us with our epistemological predicament.

Moreover, it seems that epistemic success, for humans, depends crucially on our interacting with others. Each of us needs to be open to the influence of others so as to move us from our biased, lazy conclusions to get closer to the truth. It is the social contexts of collaboration, where we must coordinate complex shared tasks, and competition, where we each have our own ideas and interests and try to convince others of them, that human reasoning properly so called takes place.

But merely being open to influence is, of course, not enough for epistemic success. Interaction with others may be required for many or most of our epistemic successes, but it also can be responsible for some of our most catastrophic epistemic failures. Conspiracy theories, group-think, echo chambers, charismatic charlatans, identity politics—these are all phenomena by which individuals can be led astray precisely by being open to the influence of others. Being epistemically successful as a human, in our particular predicament, requires being "appropriately" open to the influence of others.

If all this is at least roughly correct, it is a central feature of the HEP that we depend on interactions with others to achieve epistemic success. Our evolved cognitive apparatus, in isolation, is not likely to lead us consistently to the truth. The epistemic goods we crave, whatever

10   THE VIRTUE OF OPEN-MINDEDNESS

they may be, can be gotten only in conjunction with others. What is required is a facility with navigating the influences and perspectives of those others in order to achieve epistemic success. And this facility must take into account the limitations of our evolved cognitive apparatus. I suggest that we take this as a guide to our theorizing about open-mindedness. Open-mindedness is a virtue that makes an individual good at navigating the doxastic influences and perspectives of others so as to achieve epistemic goods. I don't propose this as a definition but more as a touchstone for guiding us toward the desiderata of a definition.

According to Jason Baehr, to be open-minded is to be able and willing to transcend one's cognitive standpoint and take up or take seriously another.[13] The devil, as always, is in the details. What is a cognitive standpoint? What is it to transcend one? How do you take one up or take it seriously? Any development of Baehr's theory will, of necessity, be addressed to these questions. But in light of the previous discussion, it is clear that a theory of open-mindedness that is to be applicable to humans as we are must ask other questions as well. "How do I know that my cognitive standpoint does not constitute a biased perspective? How can I be open-minded if I am excluded from spaces where alternative standpoints are discussed?" Given the existence of epistemic traps,[14] how do I remain open to alternative standpoints while avoiding being sucked into them? What if a standpoint seems good to me because of the influence of epistemically irrelevant or even pernicious features of my environment? Answering the first set of questions is unlikely to yield answers to the second set.

There are really at least two different ways that our theorizing might be guided by this picture. One way is to think that the very definition of open-mindedness must be revised to take account of these central features of the HEP. Perhaps we need add to, delete from, or otherwise amend Baehr's account. Indeed, my own previous work has been along these lines. In "Open-Mindedness"[15] I argued that true open-mindedness required specific kinds of self-knowledge and self-monitoring, precisely to avoid being unduly influenced by various biases one might have. In "Open-Mindedness, Insight,

INTRODUCTION 11

and Understanding"[16] I argued that Baehr's definition needed to be amended so as to prevent people who are oblivious to alternative cognitive standpoints or else too sure of their own from counting as open-minded, even if they were "willing and able" to take seriously another standpoint, if only there was one, or one that was worth considering.

Another possibility, though, is to accept the definition as a high-level normative description of what we aspire to, but recognize that approximating it might require different approaches than the most direct. For example, how to become more willing and able to take seriously an alternative cognitive standpoint? Think harder? Reflect more? No doubt that will be important. But other practices may also be useful or even indispensable that are not obviously reflected in the definition—practices that work on us at a level below reflection.

One could view much of the work in this volume as contributing to a more "ground up" approach to theorizing about open-mindedness. I don't suggest it as an alternative but rather as complementary. Baehr's definition (and others like it) provide the normative standards we crave in our epistemic terms but leaves open many questions about how real people could approximate its conditions. Lower-level descriptions of the many disparate ways real people experience, exhibit, develop, and embody open-mindedness can broaden and deepen our understanding of the phenomenon to be defined. This might include things like arranging our lives to present us with a variety of doxastic influences, or meditative practices that encourage the development of sympathetic emotions, or devising social institutions that create conditions under which being appropriately receptive to the right influences is more likely.

The chapters contained in this book pursue the task of theorizing about open-mindedness in a variety of ways, some more "top-down" and theoretical and others more "ground-up" and descriptive or practical. The hope is that exploring the territory from a variety of directions will yield an illuminating body of work that can both enrich our understanding of how people manage to be open-minded sometimes as well as help us devise the best account of what open-mindedness is that we can.

12   THE VIRTUE OF OPEN-MINDEDNESS

4 Chapters

Chapter 1 is by the philosopher Elizabeth Camp. Her contribution, "Perspectival Complacency, Perversion, and Amelioration" addresses one of the aspects of the HEP discussed already—the fact that, as individuals, we are prone to bias in our judgments and perceptions. She gives a rich and deep analysis of what she calls "perspectives," which are modes of interpretation that involve, among other things, our beliefs, values, and emotions. According to Camp, a perspective is "an open-ended disposition to interpret whatever one encounters within the perspective's target domain, but *noticing, connecting*, and *responding* to information in an intuitive way that is partly but not entirely under one's voluntary control." Such dispositions strongly influence what we believe and, of particular relevance here, how we respond to incoming information that challenges our preconceived ideas. They resist their own demise by noticing, connecting, and responding to information in ways that reinforce them and that minimize alternative interpretations.

Camp is at pains to make clear that perspectives play an invaluable role in human cognition and in framing our available information in ways that allow us to process it in real time. But it easy to see that a cognitive structure that shapes our experience and reflection so as to inherently support one interpretation at the expense of others can lead to an epistemically problematic dogmatism. Camp gives a detailed account of perspectives, and related phenomena such as frames and characterizations, articulating both the epistemic threats they represent to open-mindedness and various strategies we might pursue to mitigate those threats.

In Chapter 2, "Perspective-Taking and a Flexible Mind: A Tibetan Buddhist Approach to Open-Mindedness," the philosopher Emily McRae proposes that we look to the Tibetan Buddhist tradition to find guidance in our theorizing about open-mindedness. She examines a "mental quality" that is prized in the Buddhist Abhidharma tradition, which she calls "pliancy." While she does not claim that this is identical to the trait that is the subject of this volume, she does argue that it is a quality that is valuable for many of the same reasons that open-mindedness is taken to be valuable. Pliancy, McRae says, "is the

INTRODUCTION 13

skill of being mentally flexible enough to take up an object in order to concentrate on it. . . . Like OM [open-mindedness], pliancy is understood in Buddhist philosophy in opposition to the rigid thinking and inflexible mental habits that prevent a more accurate understanding of the world."

Importantly, McRae notes that Buddhist discussions of pliancy, unlike most contemporary discussions of open-mindedness as an epistemic virtue, tend to highlight the moral, physical, and emotional dimensions of pliancy as a mental quality. McRae gives a careful and accessible analysis of these features of pliancy, along the way providing reasons for thinking that theories of open-mindedness might benefit from making similar efforts to incorporate these insights.

Giving a brief and introductory characterization of Chapter 3, "Indigenous Tricksters' Sideways Looks at Open-Mindedness as a Virtue," by retired professor of counseling psychology Rockey Robbins and Howard Bad Hand, Lakota Sun Dance chief and healer, poses quite a challenge, as does the chapter itself, quite literally. Written in an unconventional style for academia, Robbins and Bad Hand attempt to answer the question, "What is open-mindedness" from a Native American perspective? The challenge for them is to do this in a way that is authentic even though the mode of presentation—an academic chapter—is one that historically (and presently) treats their traditional ways of knowing and of expressing themselves as "primitive" or "uncivilized." "To achieve a Native American perspective necessarily entails challenging not only . . . Western ideologies, the epistemologies and hegemonies of Western colonialism, but also the modes of expressing ideas which are also assumed by colonizers as psychologically and ideologically superior."

Robbins and Bad Hand apply a combination of methods in the chapter to accomplish this. Much of it is written in a "standard" argumentative rhetorical style, but the authors also use "Native American communicative approaches," which include storytelling and humor, among others. The editor of this volume had several collaborative meetings with Robbins but did not ask for any revisions of the authors' draft. Doing otherwise would seem to defy the spirit of the writing itself.

Chapter 4 by Emily Robertson, a philosopher of education, is entitled, "Free Speech and Challenges to Open-Mindedness in Higher Education." This chapter addresses issues that arise, not from

14 THE VIRTUE OF OPEN-MINDEDNESS

our limited cognitive powers nor from our embodiment, but from the sociality of our cognitive practices. As already discussed, each of us depends on the contributions of others to achieve epistemic success. Institutions of "higher education" play an important role in generating, preserving, and passing along information that individual students would never be able to collect on their own. But in the politically divided United States, there is controversy about what information should be taught. Students of one political team protest speakers brought to campus by the other. Politicians decry that evolution is taught as fact or that vaccines cause autism is not. Some state governments have begun legislating what subjects can and cannot be taught in state colleges and universities.

Robertson weighs in on the difficult question of how universities should honor their commitment to open-mindedness. Taking her cues about open-mindedness from several sources rather than defending a specific theory, she wades into a daunting intersection of competing interests: defending freedom of speech, supporting the pursuit of truth, protecting the socially vulnerable from harmful speech, honoring the authority of science and scholarship, and preserving academic freedom, to name a few. Universities are being forced to make decisions about curriculum, policies, and public access to information that put them at odds with one group or another no matter what they do. Though she does not find a solution, per se, to this unfortunate situation, Robertson carefully and methodically goes through the most important considerations that a solution must honor.

Peggy Garvey, a literature scholar, is the author of Chapter 5. Her contribution, "Jacques Copeau's Theatre and Masks: Actor Training as Formation in Open-Mindedness," is a kind of philosophico-biographicus. Garvey tells the story of Jacques Copeau, the founder of a theater school who "was once world-famous for having radically transformed the art of acting and enhancing its beauty." Garvey argues that Copeau has been largely misunderstood by historians who failed to acknowledge the deep influence of the work of his contemporary, Maria Montessori. According to Garvey, Copeau applied principles of the Montessori method of instruction to develop his radical new way of training actors.

INTRODUCTION 15

Among those principles were the importance of developing and maintaining a "child-like wonder" about the world and the importance of "physically adept, interest-driven movement and play." The details are complex and fascinating, but I'll mention just two major claims Garvey defends that have to do with open-mindedness. First, she argues that the combination of Montessorian and other principles Copeau weaves together into his new theater training amount to a focus on developing open-mindedness and authenticity in his actors, as opposed to what he took to be a rigid and shallow mimicry that was prevalent at the time. Second, Copeau developed theater training exercises that engaged both actors' emotions and their physical bodies in ways that he believed aided in their development of open-mindedness and authenticity.

The final chapter's title, "How to be Open-Minded: Ask Good Questions (and Listen to the Answers)," gives away what Lani Watson is up to. She addresses the practical and developmental question of how one is to become more open-minded than one is. Watson draws on her prior body of work analyzing the epistemic significance of good questioning. This chapter is an extension of that work, connecting it to the development of open-mindedness. Throughout the chapter, Watson keeps the account grounded by first describing and then frequently alluding to the real-life case of Daniella Young, who was first indoctrinated into a cult and then escaped, both physically and psychologically. Young's experience of opening her mind from the rigid dogma of the cult she was raised in provides a window onto the position Watson argues for.

Watson adopts Jason Baehr's definition of open-mindedness which characterizes it partly in terms of the transcendence of a "default cognitive standpoint." Baehr does not say much about what such transcendence looks like, but Watson draws both from his text and her own analysis to characterize it in more detail. She argues that transcendence should be thought of primarily as an activity rather than a state, and that the best way of understanding that activity renders the practice of "good questioning" as an instance of such activity. Hence, asking good questions is seen to be a way of engaging in the relevant form of transcendence of a default cognitive standpoint. This allows Watson to

16 THE VIRTUE OF OPEN-MINDEDNESS

draw on her work describing how to ask good questions as a way also to help develop open-mindedness.

5 Conclusion

The essays in this volume range widely over the landscape of open-mindedness. None of them poses a full theory of the virtue, but all make contributions to our understanding of what is required from such a theory. Several themes emerge in line with the methodological view expressed at the beginning of this introduction. (Again, I stress that these remarks in no way suggest that the authors subscribe to this methodological view.) Many of the essays stress the perspectival and biased nature of our pictures of the world or some domain within it. This is most overt in Camp's chapter, in which she anatomizes in rigorous detail some of the ways our thoughts are encoded that constitute such bias. But it is present in other chapters as well. The problem of how to (or whether) to police free speech on college campuses, as discussed by Robertson, arises, in part, because people become entrenched in political views and identities that screen them off from a reasonable consideration of the views of others. The method of good questioning elucidated by Watson is designed precisely to allow us to transcend the default cognitive standpoints that we are prone to get stuck in. And Robbins's and Bad Hand's chapter attempts to show how colonization threatens to trap the colonized within the perspective of the colonizers, perhaps the most totalizing and challenging example of the cognitive power of perspectives.

But there are other points of contact as well. The role of affect in our ability to be open to alternative standpoints was surprisingly prevalent. The Camp, Garvey, McCrae, and Robbins and Bad Hand chapters all discuss how being open-minded involved either having a certain affect or else stressed the importance of affect in helping one become more open-minded. Not unrelatedly, those same essays stress the embodiedness of our cognition as well. For instance, the Tibetan Buddhist idea of "pliancy," which McRae argues overlaps considerably with Western ideas of open-mindedness, has an explicitly physical dimension to it. And the practice of covering one's face with a mask is a

INTRODUCTION 17

physical act that Garvey tells us Copeau pioneered to help his theater students get away from identification with their selves so they could become someone else more convincingly. Both the physical covering of the face and the physical sensation of seeing others masked played a part in this practice.

And finally, there is the social dimension of open-mindedness. Robertson's chapter addresses directly the question of how our public institutions of higher education should intersect with the goals of encouraging open-mindedness among our students. Selman et al. similarly address this question within pedagogy at earlier stages of education. And Watson's entire premise of how to be open-minded is inherently social in application. In order to ask good questions, we must interact with others. We literally cannot develop open-mindedness this way without other people.

Notes

1. Matthew Chrisman, 2021, *Belief, Agency, and Knowledge* (Oxford: Oxford University Press), 2.
2. Chrisman, *Belief*, 6.
3. I have in mind here the rich relevant literatures in philosophy of race, feminist epistemology, feminist philosophy of science, etc.
4. The point being made here might be captured by the idea of "non-ideal theory." See, e.g., Charles Mills, 2017, *Black Rights/White Wrongs* (Oxford: Oxford University Press), 72–90. As I understand that notion, a non-ideal theory begins with a conception of the phenomenon to be investigated that takes pains not to abstract away from features of it that might have hidden relevance. (Of course, often the "hiddenness" is usually due more to the silencing of certain voices that have been pointing out those features than to anything intrinsically "invisible" about them.) I will be proceeding in that spirit here.
5. See, e.g., Heidi Grasswick, 2004, "Individuals-in-Communities: The Search for a Feminist Model of Epistemic Subjects," *Hypatia* 19(3): 85–86.
6. It is important to note that the epistemic value of these tendencies is not entirely negative. There are efficiency gains from some of them that might outweigh the lack of transparency and control.
7. Hugo Mercier and Dan Sperber, 2017, *The Enigma of Reason* (Cambridge, MA: Harvard University Press).
8. Mercier and Sperber, *Enigma*, 2.
9. Mercier and Sperber, *Enigma*, 4.
10. Mercier and Sperber, *Enigma*, 10.
11. Steven Sloman and Philip Fernbach, 2017, *The Knowledge Illusion* (New York: Riverhead Books).
12. Sloman and Fernbach, *The Knowledge Illusion*, 111.
13. Jason Baehr, 2011, *The Inquiring Mind: On Intellectual Virtues and Virtue Epistemology* (Oxford: Oxford University Press).

18   THE VIRTUE OF OPEN-MINDEDNESS

14. See Thi Nguyen, 2022, "Playfulness versus Epistemic Traps," in *Social Virtue Epistemology*, ed. Mark Alfano, Colin Klein, and Jeroen de Ridder (New York: Routledge).

15. Wayne Riggs, 2010, "Open-Mindedness," in *Virtue and Vice: Moral and Epistemic*, ed. Heather Battaly (Malden, MA: Wiley-Blackwell).

16. Wayne Riggs, 2016, "Open-Mindedness, Insight, and Understanding," in *Intellectual Virtues in Education: Essays in Applied Virtue Epistemology*, ed. Jason Baeh (New York: Routledge).

1

Perspectival Complacency, Perversion, and Amelioration

Elisabeth Camp

1 Perspectives as Double-Edged Swords

Talk of perspectives is everywhere: in politics, art, and our personal lives, we speak of transforming our "outlook," of articulating our "vision" or "worldview," of suddenly getting someone's "point of view."[1] Such talk is not idle: clashes and shifts of perspective are an undeniable feature of our individual and social realities. But it is difficult to know what such talk amounts to. At a minimum, it must be metaphorical, given that it is frequently applied to non-perceptual domains. Worse, the target phenomenon is abstract and amorphous in a way that makes it exceedingly difficult to pin down.

It is also not clear whether perspectives are something we should embrace or shun. On the one hand, they perform a valuable cognitive role. Acquiring a perspective enables us to "know our way about" (Wittgenstein 1953): to assimilate new information smoothly into our network of beliefs and to respond fluidly to new situations. It also streamlines interpersonal communication and planning. On the other hand, this flexible, intuitive understanding also makes perspectives dangerously self-effacing and self-reinforcing, blinding us to interpretive limitations and luring us into interpretive complacency.

If perspectives are double-edged swords, what should we do? I will argue that as limited cognitive agents navigating a complex environment, we need perspectives. Although their flexible, intuitive nature risks seducing us into self-perpetuating prejudice, we can train our perspectival habits to conform more closely to our endorsed

Elisabeth Camp, *Perspectival Complacency, Perversion, and Amelioration* In: *The Virtue of Open-Mindedness and Perspective.* Edited by: Wayne D. Riggs, Oxford University Press.
© Oxford University Press 2025. DOI: 10.1093/9780190080723.003.0002

20   THE VIRTUE OF OPEN-MINDEDNESS

principles. However, this leaves open the possibility that those principles themselves are corrupt, in ways we cannot discern from the inside.

The best way to combat myopia and complacency, I will claim, is to enrich our range of perspectival resources, especially through framing devices like art and history. However, I will also argue that exposure to alien perspectives risks perverting our endorsed perspective. From the inside, we cannot distinguish perversion from enlightenment; but we lack access to any neutral point from which to adjudicate between perspectives. Our best option, I conclude, is to cultivate a resilient perspectival flexibility while critically probing perspectives for aptness through logic and conversation.

To see why perspectives carry these risks and rewards and to understand how best to manage them, we need a clearer sense of what perspectives are. In §2, I sketch such an account and identify how perspectives differ from beliefs and other propositional attitudes. I present the threat of perspectival complacency in §3, the antidote of perspectival open-mindedness in §4, and its commensurate risk of perspectival perversion in §5. In §6, I sketch some internal and external norms for assessing perspectival aptness. Although there are no reliable recipes for improving aptness, I conclude in §7 by exploring some tools for perspectival amelioration.

2 What Even Is a Perspective?

Perspectives are ubiquitous, but also tacit and amorphous. Moreover, different theorists deploy the term 'perspective' to refer to overlapping but distinct phenomena. To focus discussion, it is helpful to begin with some relatively concrete examples.

2.1 Some Touchstone Cases

Politics starkly showcases perspectival variation. Two people encounter largely overlapping information about an event—say, a police shooting; an increase in the stock market or the murder rate; a rule for or against wearing masks or headscarves. But they draw dramatically

PERSPECTIVAL COMPLACENCY, PERVERSION 21

different conclusions about why that event occurred, what it portends, and how one should feel and act in response. Further, these different responses are systematically correlated with divergent responses to many other situations. With enough research and debate, the two individuals may come to agree about all the local claims under discussion. But they still fail to see "eye-to-eye", insofar as the relevant difference is located in a deeper nexus of assumptions and values. We observe a similar perspectival inflection in religious difference: thus, Catholics, evangelical Christians, Unitarian Universalists, Hasidic Jews, Confucians, Zen Buddhists, Hindus, Sunni and Shiite Muslims, and New Age enthusiasts differ in their doctrinal commitments and in their moral judgments and affective responses to particular behaviors; but these particular differences matter and persist insofar as they exemplify deeper differences in what those religions assume and advocate about how people should act in the world.

A salient feature of both political and religious perspectives is that they are deeply suffused with value. But perspectival variation is also evident in science, where moral and aesthetic values are less overtly on display. Thus, in microeconomics we might contrast a rational choice approach with a behavioral one (Mathis and Stefen 2015): the two "paradigms" have different explanatory targets, make different empirical assumptions about human minds, and idealize away from those assumptions in different ways. Similarly, in anthropology we might contrast androcentric and gynocentric approaches to the evolution of tool use in early hominids (Longino and Doell 1983) in terms of which environmental pressures were most pressing, which innovations occurred first, and what causal effects they produced.

As these examples illustrate, part of what makes perspectives difficult to adjudicate, even in science, is that substantive assumptions are intimately intertwined with values and priorities. In particular, scientific paradigms often trade off explanatory virtues like breadth, depth, and precision in different ways.

Most scientific perspectives are also like political and religious perspectives in being explicitly articulated and institutionally regulated. By contrast, many everyday perspectives are more individual, tacit, and unregimented. For instance, we might contrast a detail-oriented, problem-solving approach to life with a romantic,

22 THE VIRTUE OF OPEN-MINDEDNESS

meaning-seeking one; or a hierarchical, boundary-setting perspective on parenting with an egalitarian, nurturing one.

Nuanced perspectival variation is especially evident in fiction (Camp 2017a). Thus, Margaret Mitchell's *Gone with the Wind* expresses a nostalgic, white-oriented perspective on the antebellum slave-owning South, while Alice Randall's parody *The Wind Done Gone* focalizes its Black inhabitants. Fictions like Akira Kurosawa's *Rashomon*, Henry James's *Turn of the Screw*, and Vladimir Nabokov's *Lolita* and *Pale Fire* make perspectival variation their focal subject matter; while films like M. Night Shyamalan's *Sixth Sense*, David Fincher's *Fight Club,* and Christopher Nolan's *Inception* employ plot twists that retrospectively transform our perspectives on their narrated events.

These political, religious, scientific, personal, and artistic examples vary widely—most obviously, in their domains of application and their factual and normative commitments, but also in their breadth of application, their intrapersonal and interpersonal stability, and in their intellectual, evaluative, imagistic, and emotional involvement. This massively multi-dimensional heterogeneity might make it appear quixotic to theorize about perspectives as a unified kind. Against this, I want to suggest that at an appropriate level of abstraction, these variations can be seen as exemplifying a common functional role that generates a distinctive common profile of epistemic risks and benefits. Further, this functional role suggests a common set of epistemic norms for assessing perspectival aptness and a common set of techniques for ameliorating their limitations.

I don't intend to lay claim to the unique definition of perspectives as a natural kind. Other theorists have proposed their own analyses, and will want to pick and choose among the various elements of this functional role or add further elements depending on their theoretical needs. Further, the differences in domain, stability, and cognitive resources I propose to abstract away from do have significant effects. What I claim is that the suite of cognitive operations I identify work together in a functionally coherent way, which is discernibly operative in the touchstone cases that should guide our theorizing about perspectives in the relevant sense.

In the remainder of this section, I offer a brief sketch of this common functional role. In short, a perspective as I understand it, is an open-ended disposition to interpret whatever one encounters within the perspective's target domain, by *noticing, connecting,* and *responding* to information in an intuitive way that is partly but not entirely under one's voluntary control. Applied to some particular topic, a perspective synthesizes a complex body of information into a rich, holistic, multi-dimensional construal, which I call a *characterization*. The most obvious instances are stereotypes of social kinds, like women or Republicans. But where stereotypes are culture-wide ways of thinking about types, characterizations also include idiosyncratic construals of particular persons, objects, and events, such as one's colleague, childhood home, or planned wedding. And while many characterizations are like stereotypes in including vivid images and affective attitudes, we also have characterizations of abstract subjects like economics and consequentialism. Finally, where stereotypes have particular targets, perspectives are open-ended dispositions to form and update characterizations for any target in a domain.

We sometimes express perspectives through *frames*: representational vehicles that crystallize a perspective into a focal interpretive principle. Familiar types of frame include metaphors, like "Juliet is the sun" (Camp 2006, 2017b); slurs and other social labels, like "slut" or "queer" (Camp 2013, 2018; Camp and Flores 2024); mantras and memes, like "He's just not that into you" or "Minds are computers" (Camp 2020); and generics like "Women are cooperative" or "Boys will be boys" (Leslie 2008; Haslanger 2015). As these examples illustrate, frames can connect to perspectives and to the world in many different ways. But they all function as frames insofar as they stabilize perspectives by associating them with concrete, intuitively resonant representational types that can be re-tokened across contexts and agents.

In §2.2 through §2.4, I expand briefly on how perspectives affect interpretation by influencing what information we notice, and how we connect and respond to it.

2.2 Attention and Prominence

The first way that perspectives affect interpretation is by guiding how we initially encounter and process the world. Although we experience

24 THE VIRTUE OF OPEN-MINDEDNESS

ourselves as directly accessing a detailed, integrated reality, it is empirically indisputable that our engagement with the world is highly selective, and that what agents notice and how they encode it is affected by their background assumptions and purposes. For current purposes, it's useful to distinguish three more specific respects in which perspectives affect attention.[2]

First, attention *parses* situations into objects and features of repeatable types, which are connected and distinguished within a complex network of categorical distinctions, or a taxonomy (Carnap 1928/1967; Rosch 1976). This taxonomy itself presupposes that those categories are grounded in lower-level features, at least in the sense that those lower-level features cluster together in relatively stable patterns (Boyd 1999). I'll call the parsed features in terms of which an agent intuitively encodes and thinks about the topics they interpret—typically features like being a human, a car, a man, or fast, middle-class, or threatening—*basic* features.[3] By using a taxonomy to parse the world, an agent presupposes that its categories track basic features that *matter*, at least in the sense of being relevant to the agent's goals. An agent may parse basic features by being sensitive to patterns among lower-level features without being able to explicitly identify those lower-level features or patterns in themselves: for instance, they may intuitively code someone as male, middle-class, or threatening without being able to articulate why.

Second, attention *selects* some parsed features for conscious awareness. The influence of an agent's interests and purposes on selection is famously illustrated by the "invisible gorilla": an actor in a gorilla suit who walks through a group and is unnoticed by most test subjects who are tasked with counting the group's basketball passes but completely obvious to subjects not assigned that task (Simons and Chabris 1999). Although the invisible gorilla illustrates top-down effects on selection, unexpected features and objects can also intrude into awareness from the bottom up.

Third, within those features that are consciously recognized, attention allocates greater *prominence* to some than others. Following Tversky (1977), I understand prominence (which he calls "salience") as a function of two distinct but mutually influencing factors: intensity and diagnosticity.

PERSPECTIVAL COMPLACENCY, PERVERSION   25

Intense features have a high signal-to-noise ratio. In simple cases, like a lightbulb's illumination, a feature's intensity can be specified in terms of a physical departure from its local surrounding conditions. However, in many cases the interaction between context and intensity is more complex, insofar as what counts as irrelevant "noise" or as a departure from the feature's expected magnitude itself depends on the agent's background assumptions. Thus, to art historians, the intensity of a patch of pigment will depend not just on its saturation level relative to that of surrounding patches but also on their assumptions about typical saturation levels for other paintings within that genre and in other genres. Such background statistical assumptions also modulate non-perceptual assignments of intensity. For instance, the property of being a Republican will likely be more intense in an agent's thinking about George if they know him through playing Ultimate Frisbee, and employ a culturally entrenched stereotype of Ultimate players as crunchy liberals, than if they know him from the golf course where they expect to find Republicans.

Where intensity is essentially contrastive, *diagnosticity* is essentially connective: it allocates attention to features that are classificatorily useful, because they are purportedly correlated with other features that are relevant given the agent's purposes. So, for instance, subtle details about the color, pattern, and placement of a man's handkerchief or tie might be diagnostic of his affiliation with and status within a social group. Like intensity, assignments of diagnosticity are often richly mediated by an agent's background assumptions: for instance, a patch of ultramarine blue will be especially prominent to someone who knows that it was produced with lapis lazuli, which was often used to signify the wealth of the painting's commissioning patron.

The overall prominence of a given feature in an agent's intuitive thinking is a combined function of its assigned intensity and diagnosticity. Intensity and diagnosticity are often aligned, whether by natural or artificial design: thus, poison frogs and stop signs are both bright red because the highly intense color draws attention to highly relevant information. But the two can come apart. Thus, a flashing light may pull your gaze even if you know it is just a child's toy; and a snake's triangular head shape and vertically elliptical pupils may be highly noticeable to someone who knows that those features are correlated with snakes' being venomous, even if those features are not themselves large or brightly marked.

To the extent that background taxonomic and statistical assumptions and purposes drive encoding and recall, by influencing how agents parse, select, and prioritize the information they encounter, we should predict that agents with different taxonomies, assumptions, and purposes will process equivalent information in systematically different ways. Moreover, there is an important sense in which different taxonomies, assumptions, and purposes *warrant* attending to different profiles of features. The bedeviling question, to which we'll turn in §6, is how to adjudicate which profile of assumptions and purposes an agent should employ. In the remainder of this section, I discuss the two other main ways that perspectives affect agents' intuitive handling of information: connection, and response.

2.3 Connection and Centrality

Perspectival interpretation isn't merely a matter of encoding a list of informational bits, even a curated list prioritized by prominence. Agents assimilate the information they select and prioritize into complex networks, so that some features are more *central* in their intuitive thinking. A decent measure of a feature's cognitive centrality is its "mutability": how much the agent's overall intuitive thinking about the topic would change if they no longer attributed that feature to it (Murphy and Medin 1985; Thagard 1989; Sloman, Love, and Ahn 1998).

Features can be connected on a wide variety of grounds. The simplest connection is a pure conditioned association, such as the sound of a bell and the smell of food (Pavlov 1927) or the taste of a cookie and the memory of a gauzy curtain (Proust 1913). However, most intuitive connections have some putatively justificatory status, such that the presence of one feature *motivates* attributing the other. While some such connections, like that between bachelors being unmarried and their being male, or between being a squirrel and being furry, may be purely conceptual or metaphysical, most of the connections that drive our intuitive cognition are more contingent. For instance, many of us intuitively expect bachelors to live in small urban apartments, socialize frequently, and drink lots of alcohol. Some of these imputed correlations are assigned a causal basis; while others are moral—say, that bachelors deserve to be lonely because they never learned to practice genuine empathy; or aesthetic—say, that bachelors should furnish their apartments with leather couches and chrome lamps because this embodies their tough, glamorous lifestyle.

The imputed connecting grounds just invoked are obviously quite different. One hallmark of perspectivally driven thought is that we intuitively take some features to "fit" together with each other and with the subject to which they're attributed, without being clear about *why* they fit. Further, when we are prompted to clarify, we often impute stronger grounds than our evidence warrants: for instance, attributing a general, normatively inflected metaphysical basis for an isolated observed correlation. I return to these risks of overinterpretation in §3. For the purpose of sketching perspectives' effects on intuitive thought, it suffices to note three points. First, regardless of their putative basis, features that are more centrally connected are thereby more accessible for recall and more influential in accessing and explaining other features. Second, agents with different practical and theoretical purposes and different factual assumptions about how and why features are distributed both *will* and *should* connect the same set of features into distinct patterns. And third, as with intensity and diagnosticity, prominence and centrality are often aligned but can come apart.

2.4 Prediction, Evaluation, and Response

So far, we've seen that agents with different perspectives operate with different categories, statistical assumptions, and purposes. As a result, they will not be merely disposed to but internally justified in selecting and prioritizing different features for attention and recall, and in connecting these features together into different patterns on different grounds. In turn, these different interpretations of the situations they encounter

28 THE VIRTUE OF OPEN-MINDEDNESS

will prime them to form different expectations about what else is true of and will happen in those situations. For instance, a Fox-News-watching Republican and an NPR-listening Democrat who both know that George is a bachelor who plays golf and Ultimate Frisbee are likely to make different predictions about George's job, car, food preferences, and religious affiliations, or about how he would respond to a report of vandalism during a protest over a police killing of a Black man.

In addition to straightforwardly informational differences, agents with different perspectives will *color* the features they impute in different evaluative terms: morally, aesthetically, and emotionally. Thus, someone who prioritizes family relations might pity a bachelor for spending so many hours alone while someone who prioritizes self-sufficiency might celebrate his social freedom. These specific evaluations of particular constituent features affect an agent's evaluation of other constituent features, as well as their evaluation of the overall topic. Thus, pity for George's solitary time might be linked to contempt for the hours he spends alone at the gym and to an overall feeling of alienation toward him.

Coloring often goes deeper than layering a normative value onto a neutral informational base; rather, the basic parsing and attribution of features intertwines description and evaluation in an indissoluble, holistic way (McDowell 1981; Williams 1985). That is, an agent's interpreting some encountered situation as one in which a subject S possesses a basic feature F often depends on their background assumptions about the statistical distributions among a complex network of further basic and lower-level features, which are themselves normatively loaded. For instance, the same motion might be perceived as a playful invitation or as a threat, or the same utterance might be perceived as jocular "locker room talk" or as a demeaning insult, depending on the ascribing agent's assumptions about who is acting or speaking and about how people of various social categories tend to and should engage in social bonding.

Different ways of parsing a situation afford and motivate different responses to it (Gibson 1979; McClelland and Sliwa 2023). Thus, an agent who hears an utterance as locker room banter might find George compellingly zany and be motivated to approach him and other

PERSPECTIVAL COMPLACENCY, PERVERSION 29

bachelors at a party; while an agent who hears the utterance as an insult might find George threateningly misogynistic and be motivated to avoid him and his "bro" friends.

Finally, an agent's perspective systematically influences their intuitive thinking, not just about one particular subject or feature but about a range of other topics. Thus, at least in the United States, an agent's intuitive characterizations of George, locker rooms, social banter, and bachelors are likely to cohere with their characterizations of unmarried women, fathers, grandmothers, noisy bars, motorcycles, and detached houses with lawns, among other things. To the extent that these various distinct characterizations are driven by a common taxonomy; common statistical assumptions; and common moral, aesthetic, and practical values, they cohere into a broadly encompassing, mutually supporting interpretive network.

2.5 Perspectives and Propositions

Much of the impetus for invoking perspectives is to contrast them with standard propositional attitudes like belief. What light can the above analysis of perspectives as dispositions to notice, connect, and respond to information can shed on this contrast?

The first major contrast is that perspectives are not particular attitudes or representations but modes of interpreting whatever situations an agent encounters within the perspective's domain of application. In a slogan, perspectives are *tools* for thought rather than thoughts per se. As we have seen, they are not devoid of content: they presuppose a taxonomy, which embodies statistical assumptions, values, and priorities. These presuppositions can be articulated in propositional terms. But they are so fundamental that they function more like conditions on the possibility of making cuts in a space of possibilities (Stalnaker 2014) than as such cuts themselves.

Moreover, perspectives can guide interpretation without being associated with any particular set of focal beliefs. Many perspectives, like liberalism or nationalism, lack substantive, defining propositional commitments; instead, they are rooted in a nexus of expectations and

30   THE VIRTUE OF OPEN-MINDEDNESS

values that can be flexibly filled out with a wide range of more fine-grained assumptions. Other perspectives are plausibly defined by specific doctrines: for instance, evangelical Protestantism canonically requires commitment to the Bible's inerrancy and to Jesus's divinity as the only route to eternal life. However, what makes such doctrinal propositions perspectivally relevant, when they are, is their functional role in guiding intuitive interpretation; and they can perform this function in the absence of the sort of endorsement characteristic of belief. Indeed, most evangelical Christians today believe that salvation is possible without belief in Jesus's divinity.[4] Similarly, many devotees of astrology disavow causal connections between stars' positions and personalities. What makes these people adherents of their respective perspectives is not acceptance of any particular content but their commitment to construing the world in the relevant way. Indeed, as we'll see in a moment, a perspective can guide one's intuitive thinking even when one does not endorse it as the appropriate way to construe the world.

To say that perspectives are tools for thought might just mean that they govern the *dynamics* of thought, where this is compatible with their output being straightforwardly propositional attitudes like belief (or desire or intention). We can pinpoint the difference between propositional attitudes and perspectives more directly by comparing beliefs with characterizations, as the outputs of perspectives, and noting that one can intuitively "get" a characterization, in the sense of being able to instantiate the relevant intuitive dispositions, without believing it. For instance, I "get" the stereotypical characterization of bachelors without believing that it is factually accurate or normatively valid. Likewise, our attention is regularly drawn to features, like skin color, that we would rather ignore; and we often intuitively associate features, like attractiveness and intelligence, that we don't reflectively believe are causally connected or even robustly correlated.[5] Conversely, we often *fail* to "get" characterizations whose contents we reflectively endorse, as on first encounter with a scientific or social theory (Camp 2020). In general, it is neither necessary nor sufficient for getting a characterization that one entertain, endorse, or otherwise explicitly represent a set of propositions specifying its contents.

PERSPECTIVAL COMPLACENCY, PERVERSION   31

Rather, I suggest that "getting" a characterization requires it to be easily *implemented* in an agent's intuitive thinking. Implementation entails, first, that when the agent thinks about the relevant topic, the basic features that are attributed by that characterization are spontaneously activated in cognition. In particular, the agent must be disposed to represent experiential features in a phenomenologically vivid way and be disposed to be motivated by morally, aesthetically, emotionally, and practically valenced features. Intuitive implementation entails that in cases where the agent does not reflectively believe that the subject actually possesses a feature attributed by the characterization, they must expend some cognitive effort to avoid deploying it in their thinking.

Second, intuitive implementation entails that the characterization's higher-order structural properties of prominence and centrality are also instantiated within the agent's cognitive architecture, so that the agent is actually disposed to notice and recall prominent features and to draw a rich range of inferences about highly diagnostic features and central features.

In these respects, "getting" a characterization is analogous to getting a perceptual Gestalt. It is not sufficient to see Figure 1 as an old lady to look at it while endorsing the proposition that the concept *old lady* applies to it. Trying to apply the concept often helps, but does not guarantee success. If and when the concept does lock into one's perception, the figure's disparate elements are subsumed into a coherently structured whole on which certain features are especially prominent, take on a certain significance, and are connected to others in certain ways. And this structure and significance is markedly different from that produced by seeing the figure as a young lady, or as a meaningless jumble.

So too for "getting" a non-perceptual characterization: implementation makes a phenomenological and functional difference that cannot be reduced to entertaining or endorsing a certain set of contents. Thus, a student who gets the characterizations of "jocks" and "burnouts" operative at an American high school will notice, recall, explain, predict, and respond to a wide range of features and behaviors in real time in a way that someone who simply acquires an understanding of those characterizations from reading a sociolinguistics text, like Eckert

Figure 1. William Ely Hill, *My wife and my mother-in-law. They are both in this picture—find them.* Illustration in *Puck* 78(2018) (November 6, 1915): 11. Courtesy of the Library of Congress Prints and Photographs Division. PD-US.

(2000), may not. An agent—say, a teacher—might be intuitively competent with those characterizations without endorsing them; and both teachers and students might be capable of switching to a different set of characterizations—say, "college prep" and "vocational"—which dispose them to notice, explain, and respond to the same set of people and behaviors quite differently.

PERSPECTIVAL COMPLACENCY, PERVERSION   33

This distinction between propositionally entertaining or endorsing and intuitively "getting" extends from particular characterizations to perspectives at large. Thus, on the one hand, a scientist might possess an ideal Carnapian specification of a discipline's paradigm or conceptual scheme—comprised of its taxonomy, statistical assumptions, and values and priorities—but be unable to put that specification to work in characterizing situations as they arise in real time. Conversely, a committed feminist might be disposed, while immersed in reading *Bridget Jones's Diary* or *Fifty Shades of Grey*, to construe particular fictional characters and the world more generally in terms of a gender ideology that they reflectively reject and which they do not deploy in most other environments, such as applying for jobs or using a dating app.

3 Perspectival Complacency

The sketch of perspectives in §2 puts us in a position to begin explaining perspectives' double-edged interpretive effects. As limited agents navigating a complex world, we need perspectives: they are essential for encoding and accessing information in ways that reflect our purposes and values, so that we can act fluidly, flexibly, and appropriately in response (Camp 2019). At the same time, these very features also make perspectives prone to distortion. Further, as open-ended, flexible dispositions to generate intuitive, holistic, cognitive structures, perspectives are distinctively difficult to diagnose, define, and assess.

3.1 Stereotype Accuracy and Characterizational Confirmation

Stereotype-driven thinking vividly demonstrates how perspectives can be deeply habituated, smoothly functional, and internally justified—and yet also, as Endre Begby (2013) says, "epistemically pernicious." Social kind terms like "woman," "Black," and "queer" function as perspectival frames (Camp and Flores 2024). More specifically, they express interpretive principles that render a wide range of fine-grained, superficially observable features, like skin color, dress, and

34 THE VIRTUE OF OPEN-MINDEDNESS

speech, highly *prominent* because they are (purportedly) *diagnostic* of simple, sharply defined categories. These categories are in turn treated as highly *central*: justifying inference to a wide range of unobserved features that are (purportedly) "normal" for members of that kind. "Normalcy" here entails that those features are (purportedly) differentially correlated with group membership. But it also typically entails that certain normative responses—moral, aesthetic, emotional, and/ or practical—are (purportedly) *warranted*, so that non-conformity is not merely surprising but somehow wrong. Further, for many agents, these categories are central in the sense of *explaining* group members' (purported) tendency to possess those features, in virtue of metaphysical *essences* (Haslam et al. 2000; Gelman 2005; Leslie 2014).

Many of us take stereotype-driven thinking to be insidious. Even so, we need to understand why it is compelling for those who endorse it; why even those who reject it are still prone to engage in it; and how it exemplifies risks and benefits endemic to perspectives more generally. One reason stereotypes are intuitively powerful, even for those who reflectively reject them, is that they are *self-effacing*: they lurk ubiquitously in the background, regulating parsing, selection, explanation, and response in ways that are prior to and largely below the sorts of conscious attitudes we typically articulate and dispute about. In particular, it is experimentally challenging to identify independent, objective criteria for assessing stereotypes' accuracy because both in-group and out-group individuals tend to parse the personal character traits they ascribe to individual people in stereotype-conforming terms (Judd and Park 1993). Similarly for behaviors: the same arm movement is more likely to be parsed as a playful swat or a threatening jab depending on the ascribing agent's stereotype of the race of the person performing it (Duncan 1976).

Stereotypes are also intuitively powerful because they are practically and epistemically *self-reinforcing*. In practical terms, the fact that personal traits are typically expected, recognized and responded to by others in stereotype-conforming terms sets up external "looping effects" under which it becomes increasingly efficient to act and to interpret others in terms of that stereotype (Hacking 1995, Camp and Flores 2024). All agents need to be competent with stereotypes in order to efficiently navigate such a social environment. Further, even members of groups who are subordinated by them can have good reason to conform in order to facilitate achieving their practical goals. But given this, it is cognitively efficient to use those stereotypes to regulate one's own internal expectations and responses, because it reduces the processing load imposed by maintaining the multiple ledgers of a stereotype-resisting "double consciousness" (Du Bois 1903).

In epistemic terms, stereotypes are self-reinforcing because their intuitive, sub-conscious effects invite forms of reflective justification that are distinctively difficult to disprove. First, culturally competent social agents inevitably encode significant stereotype-supporting evidence through direct encounters with, testimony about, and cultural depictions of stereotype-conforming individuals. Indeed, considered simply as statistical judgments (e.g., "What proportion of Asian-Americans complete college?"), stereotypes are arguably often fairly accurate.[6] Second, because most stereotypes ascribe a host of features on a variety of grounds, disproving the applicability of any one feature or connection among features still leaves the bulk of the stereotype intact. Third, because stereotypes have generic force, evidence of a low differential correlation between a stereotypical feature f and membership in group G need not falsify attribution of f to any particular member of G or to Gs in general. After all, generics like "Mosquitoes carry West Nile virus" are often judged true despite recognized low correlation (Leslie 2008); and even non-generic assumptions of statistical correlation and connecting grounds allow for exceptions. In particular, because the essences that purportedly ground stereotype-conforming features are deep and multi-tracked, it is possible for them to manifest in multiple ways or be masked altogether without being falsified. And even when a particular putative ground between being G and possessing f is disproven, the intuitive fittingness of the association often leads agents to seek out alternative justifications for that connection.

Given all these ways in which stereotypes are practically and epistemically self-effacing and self-reinforcing, it should not be surprising that stereotypes are as "sticky" as they are. Even so, they are deeply problematic. Most obviously, they can lead agents to posit non-existent essences, to accept unjust norms, and to perpetuate oppressive social structures. But they also lead agents into more narrowly informational

36   THE VIRTUE OF OPEN-MINDEDNESS

error, by overestimating differential correlations between properties and underestimating properties' variance within a population (Ryan et al. 1996); and by ignoring or denying individual members' nonconforming properties.

Stereotypes offer an especially crisp illustration of perspectives' self-effacing and self-reinforcing nature because they are comparatively crude and rigid, and because many of us are on the lookout for their distortions. Other characterizations—of colleagues, politicians, towns, musical genres, scientific topics, and so on—are also self-effacing and self-reinforcing. But their greater nuance, flexibility, and idiosyncrasy makes their distorting effects even harder to notice and test.

With effort and luck, some such distortions can be discerned from the inside, at least in principle. Thus, we might notice that we have been making inconsistent predictions: say, that we are surprised when a mom but not a dad we meet at school dropoff wearing scrubs turns out to be a doctor rather than a nurse, even though we know that a majority of doctors under forty-five are female. We might notice that we have been taking inconsistent actions: say, that we tend to discipline Black and brown boys in our classroom for being "disruptive" while tolerating similar behavior from white boys (and all girls) as "fidgeting." Or we might realize that we have inconsistently implemented our avowed values: say, that loving our neighbor means dropping our long-waged war against their children's trampling of our flower beds.

The work of bringing one's intuitive characterizations and one's reflective beliefs into alignment is as important as it is difficult. However, even if it is accomplished, there remain many cases of what many external observers would classify as informational and/or normative inconsistency that are internally invisible to the agent themselves. Worse, some of these inconsistencies are invisible to them, not because they fail to notice that the two features or situations are different, but because they reasonably treat the interpretive difference as justified. Consistency treats like cases alike; but there are almost always variations between cases that can be leveraged to justify distinct assessments of otherwise similar phenomena, as when one agent or different agents classify one public event as a riot and another as a protest. Inconsistency is a risk for all forms of representation, including straightforward propositional attitudes. But the rich, multi-dimensional, holistic nature of characterizations exacerbates the danger of internally justified but objectively unwarranted inconsistency significantly.

3.2 Perspectival Perpetuation

So far, I have argued that characterizations are practically and epistemically self-effacing and self-reinforcing, as illustrated by the special case of stereotypes. Turning from particular characterizations to the perspectives that generate them, we find that these qualities of self-effacement and self-reinforcement are amplified by the nature of perspectives as temporally and topically open-ended modes of interpretation.

First, with respect to attention: we can only recall, explain, and respond to information we actually notice; but we are less likely to notice information that is irrelevant for our purposes or that doesn't fit within our taxonomy, and more likely to parse clusters of lower-level features into perspective-conforming categories. By themselves, selectivity and partiality are unavoidable, functionally adaptive qualities for finite agents navigating a complex world, and needn't constitute distortion. However, we are prone to deploy attention in perspective-conforming ways that are genuinely distorting. Thus, we avoid even encountering information that fails to fit our perspectives (Nickerson 1998). When we do notice it, we tend to scrutinize it more closely, seeking reasons to dismiss it (Lord et al. 1979; Lord and Taylor 2009). And in cases where we eventually accept it, we tend to assimilate it in ways that minimize its overall effects (Anderson et al. 1980; Moreno and Bodenhausen 1999).

A similar point applies for explanation. To be prepared to act in a complex environment, finite agents must extrapolate from limited information to more general underlying structures. It is functionally adaptive to do this by imputing the most parsimonious, robust, and relevant network of connections possible. However, we are prone to turn these explanatory virtues into vices through excess. Among other things, we tend to neglect variations across contexts and extend the

38 THE VIRTUE OF OPEN-MINDEDNESS

scope of correlations too far beyond their original contexts. We tend to impute causal connections in place of mere correlation—especially when we are experiencing emotions, like anger, whose warrant requires a causal basis (Small et al. 2006). We tend to treat the causal connections we do impute as being metaphysically robust rather than superficial. And we tend to take our affective and aesthetic responses, like disgust or distaste at unfamiliar combinations of features, as evidence in favor of moral principles (Haidt and Joseph 2004).

The upshot is that perspectives must be selective, preferential, and abductive in order to perform their function of encoding, selecting, synthesizing, and responding to information in purpose-driven ways in real time. But the open-ended, intuitive, flexible, holistic nature of perspectives means that they implement selection, preference, and extrapolation in ways that tend to induce distortion and blind us to those distortions. We don't just ignore certain information and deprioritize certain values. We fail to notice the streams of perspective-dissonant information we neglect, even as we take the streams of perspective-conforming information we do collect to support our interpretive acuity. Because perspectives are self-effacing in this open-ended way, we risk falling into *myopia*: blindness to our own interpretive blindnesses. Worse, because perspectives are open-endedly self-reinforcing, we risk compounding myopia with *complacency*: we are unmotivated to seek out additional information and values or to probe for perspectival blind spots.

Agents in the grip of a distorting perspective may thus manifest pernicious interpretive habits in ways that are epistemically invisible to them and impervious to reflective introspection. As far as they can tell, they really have extrapolated a consistent set of background assumptions from their past experiences and prioritized values. And they really are using those assumptions and values to parse new information accurately, assign it appropriate levels of intensity and diagnosticity, explain it parsimoniously, and respond to it in commensurate moral, aesthetic, emotional, and practical terms.

Such agents aren't motivated to seek out "unknown unknowns," because they lack any positive evidence that they're failing to notice something they should care about. Their explanatory networks are sufficiently rich and complex that they can smoothly assimilate most of the new information they do notice, and explain away any apparent

PERSPECTIVAL COMPLACENCY, PERVERSION 39

counterexamples. And to top it off, the phenomenology of Gestalt understanding imbues them with an intuitive feeling of confidence that the world hangs together in a coherent, sensible way (Trout 2002). In Kuhnian terms, their paradigm functions effectively across a wide range of normal contexts. Barring a cataclysmic event, they have no reason to doubt that they have achieved a robust grip on reality.

From a different perspective, however, these agents' interpretive limitations and distortions may be glaringly obvious. Agent Y may see that X has failed to notice facts that are relevant by X's own lights, or that X has extrapolated statistical correlations beyond X's local context, or has ignored relevant contextual variations, or has imputed ungrounded explanatory connections. In some cases, if Y points out information that X has missed, this may give X good, if defeasible, reason to revise their particular characterizations or general background assumptions. However, Y's disagreement with X may be more than just informational, insofar as they take X to be employing a misguided taxonomy and/or to be motivated by malign purposes or confused priorities.

In such a situation, if X and Y attempt to resolve their disagreement about some particular topic—say, whether a certain politician will win an election, whether guns should be more tightly regulated, or whether Hamlet is driven by an Oedipal complex—the result may be a hermeneutic impasse. If both parties have managed to achieve internal perspectival consistency, then when each lobs what they take to be compelling evidence for their preferred conclusion at the other, this evidence is likely to produce a cavalier dismissal or at most a local concession. And in turn, their interlocutor's lack of a concessive response is likely to confirm their view that this interlocutor is myopic, even as their own ability to accommodate all the relevant information reinforces their own complacency. The result is a vicious cycle of increasing intrapersonal stagnation and interpersonal alienation.[7]

4 Perspectival Open-Mindedness

In §3, I argued that perspectives are selective and preferential in self-effacing, self-reinforcing ways that risk myopia and complacency. This is frustrating enough when we are mired in a perspectival dispute with

40 THE VIRTUE OF OPEN-MINDEDNESS

someone else. But it also offers a warning to ourselves: even when we feel secure in the integrity and acuity of our perspectival faculties, we may be getting things wrong at a deeper level. Indeed, the fact that many of us take our own past selves to have been myopic and complacent gives us good inductive reason to suspect our own current perspective. Is there any escape?

If we were simply saddled with our perspectives, then perhaps we could only shrug our shoulders and hope for the best. However, most adult humans do not dwell in a single monolithic context or deploy a single stable perspective. As we saw in §2, perspectives are contextually malleable in response to local shifts in statistical distributions, purposes, and priorities. They are also partly under voluntary control. Sometimes our perspectives shift despite ourselves, as when stereotype threat causes members of social groups to underperform in environments where the stereotype is rendered salient (Schmader et al. 2008; Steele 2010). But perspectival shifts can also be actively cultivated, much as with Figure 1. For instance, we can combat stereotype threat and implicit bias through cognitive "counterprograming" (Finnegan et al. 2015), by activating alternative stereotypes and focusing on individual group members' distinctive features. When internal cognitive measures don't suffice, we can change our external environments—for instance, by surrounding ourselves with frames that trigger perspectives we endorse (Gawronski and Cesario 2013; Brownstein 2016) and by breaking down oppressive social structures (Haslanger 2015).

Such strategies can help us achieve better internal harmony between our intuitive perspectives and our reflectively endorsed principles. But as we saw in §3, internal harmony is not enough to address the risk of complacent myopia. To discern and redress our interpretive blindspots, we need to enrich our perspectival resources. One obvious technique for such enrichment is travel: inhabiting an environment that manifests a different profile of statistical distributions and meeting people with different assumptions and values. However, this imposes a high logistical burden. It also may not be enough, if we just lug our habitual interpretive baggage with us. And it may not be necessary, if we can conjure alternative locales in our imagination.

PERSPECTIVAL COMPLACENCY, PERVERSION   41

Where we are actually situated often matters less than *how* we engage with the situations we encounter. And for the project of augmenting our perceptual repertoires, frames are plausibly our most powerful resource. As tangible representational vehicles that crystallize perspectives into stabilized, simplified forms, frames provide concrete, sustained principles for training ourselves into novel intuitive patterns of attention, connection, and response. Because literary fictions and movies are phenomenologically vivid and affectively rich, they constitute especially obvious candidates for perspectival learning (Camp 2017a). But many eloquent verbal and non-verbal works of history, religion, politics, and science are deeply perspectival (Camp 2020b).

Acquiring a novel perspective by way of a representational frame requires imaginative flexibility: first, to extrapolate from the frame's explicitly encoded contents to its associated characterizations; and second, to implement the relevant dispositions in an intuitive, flexible, open-ended way. This species of imagination is distinct from, though often engaged in combination with, t imaginative simulation of contents (Camp 2009). We are never guaranteed to succeed, and success is typically only partial. Still, perspectival play is something that most of us perform regularly, from curiosity and for fun as much as in a sober-minded search for epistemic or moral growth.

Cultivating novel perspectives offers important personal and social benefits. Personally, it can revise our characterizations of particular topics by leading us to notice new features, forge new connections, and construct alternative hypotheses. t can shift our global statistical assumptions and raise our awareness of structural interpretive biases. And it can train us to be flexible at a meta-level: responding to changing circumstances by modulating within our enriched repertoire of interpretive options (Nguyen 2020; Camp 2023).

Socially, cultivating novel perspectives can give us an intuitive ability to predict how the adherents of an alternative perspective will think and act. Instrumentally, this can help us to overcome a hermeneutic impasse, by equipping us to present evidence and arguments in terms that are congenial to our interlocutor. It can also enable us to navigate novel cultural milieus, and thereby unlock heretofore inaccessible social and economic capital (Morton 2014). More profoundly,

42 THE VIRTUE OF OPEN-MINDEDNESS

it can help us to understand others empathetically, in and despite their differences from ourselves (Lugones 1987; Nussbaum 2002; Smith 2019). For instance, many generations of white readers have felt that they came to viscerally understand what it's like to be a slave by reading Harriet Beecher Stowe's *Uncle Tom's Cabin*, what it's like to be Native American by reading James Fenimore Cooper's *Last of the Mohicans*, or what it's like to be a Chinese villager by reading Pearl S. Buck's *The Good Earth*.

The benefits of cultivating a novel perspective can be more than merely instrumental and its effects more than temporary. We may integrate elements of its taxonomy, explanatory principles, and values and priorities into our ongoing perspectival commitments. At the limit, we may embrace what was once an alien perspective as our own. This is the classic argument for liberal education: not that we learn any particular body of facts or set of investigative tools, but rather that open-minded engagement with multiple, divergent, disciplinary, and cultural perspectives undermines complacency, frees us from the shackles of our parochial assumptions and enables us to construct our own, authentic identities.

5 Perspectival Perversion

The argument for liberal education is compelling: open-mindedness is indeed a powerful antidote for myopic complacency. However, it also carries a correlative risk, of perversion. As I argued in §2, cultivating an alternative perspective requires actually implementing it, so that its profile of assumptions, purposes, and priorities regulates what one in fact notices and recalls; which associations one is inclined to make and on what grounds; and how one is motivated to respond, emotionally, morally, aesthetically, and practically. This goes beyond mere simulation and cannot be safely quarantined within a "pretense module," as simulationists like Goldman (1992) and Currie (1997) maintain (Camp 2017a, 2023). Moreover, because perspectives are open-ended, their effects cannot be limited to a fixed set of contents, in the way that the risk of contagion from repeated exposure to a disbelieved proposition might be.

One route to perversion is through *erosion:* unreflective habituation into new interpretive dispositions. We may think we are engaging with an alternative perspective only temporarily and instrumentally, for politeness, inquiry, or fun. And in many cases the long-term risk may be fairly minimal, as when we spend an afternoon with a bigoted uncle or a pack of faithless hedonists, or when we read *Lolita* or *Gone with the Wind*. But even so, assimilating and responding to information under a perspective's influence affects how we encode the information we acquire during that time and the habits by which we interpret other information going forward, in ways that are not straightforward to undo (Camp 2017a, 2023). And in many cases, as when we enter college or a career, our perspectival immersion is more prolonged. The more immersive and more sustained our perspectival engagement is, the harder it becomes to retain our own perspectival compass, and the more we may convince ourselves that it is best to "go along to get along" even within our own minds (Morton 2014).

Even engaging an alternative perspective for the sake of combating it can be risky. In a perspectival dispute, mere comprehension—determining the operative force and content of an interlocutor's speech acts—already requires significantly entraining to their perspective. This itself constitutes a kind of cognitive complicity. Beyond this, most of our available conversational responses also engender some sort of communicative complicity (Camp 2013, 2017b). That is, any response that targets an utterance's focal contents—even denial—still accommodates its background presuppositions, which then govern the subsequent conversation unless actively blocked (Lewis 1979, Langton 2019). But "blocking" by bringing presuppositions explicitly to the conversational center can be socially costly. Worse, it risks amplifying those presuppositions by implicitly acknowledging their contextual accessibility and social currency. Perspectival presuppositions in particular are so deep, amorphous, and open-ended that challenging them risks derailing the conversation entirely.

In such cases of such supposedly temporary and instrumental compliance, we risk becoming perverted into a new perspective while attempting to retain our "true" one. An alternative route to perversion is *seduction:* conversion to a whole new religion, scientific theory, political viewpoint, or musical genre; or just to a particular

44 THE VIRTUE OF OPEN-MINDEDNESS

characterization, say, of a colleague or movie. Such conversions often occur abruptly, with a Gestalt "click." In such cases, the agent is likely to feel they have been cured of heretofore undiagnosed myopia through enlightenment, so that everything is now revealed in its proper place. And sometimes this is indeed the correct diagnosis. But the feeling of enlightenment may itself be an illusion.

Conspiracy theories offer a stark illustration: their internal coherence makes them intellectually and phenomenologically satisfying, by tying together many disparate, puzzling facts via a simple explanation, often by positing a hidden cause. But this clarity and unity may not reflect actual causal structures and may blind us to relevant subtleties of reality (Nguyen 2021). Conversely, we can also be blinded by informational complexity and phenomenological intensity. Thus, our nuanced, visceral, empathetic experiences in reading fiction or history may convince us that we truly understand what it was like to be an African-American slave, a First Nations tribal member, or a villager in Communist China, when in fact we have at best inherited or confabulated a fantasy of what *we* would feel like in that situation (hooks 1992; Young 1997; Clavel Vásquez and Clavel-Vásquez 2023).

Whether the conversion is incremental or abrupt, grudging or enthusiastic, it opens a gap between the agent's past perspectival commitments and their present ones. To the agent, their new perspective's internal integrity and phenomenology of confidence confirm its rightness, even as their past self and their former compatriots accuse them of perversion. The problem is that there is no independent, accessible point from which to adjudicate who is right. While we can modulate among perspectives, we can never step outside of all perspectives to achieve a "sideways on" view of their relationships to the world or each other. As Alexander Nehamas (2000) puts it apropos of the seductive power of beauty,

> Spending time with such a thing, with other things like it, with other people who like it as well will have an effect on me which I cannot predict in advance. Once that effect is in place, I may have changed into someone I would not have wanted to be before I began. But I may now no longer be able to see that what I am, perhaps, is

PERSPECTIVAL COMPLACENCY, PERVERSION 45

perverted. How can I tell if I have followed the right course? Which standards should I apply to myself?

Thus, given that open-mindedness is in itself simply a disposition to try on alternative perspectives, and as such one that ineluctably carries the risk of perversion, we need to temper our celebration of liberal education from §4: without some further constraint, open-mindedness cannot be straightforwardly counted as a virtue.

6 Assessing Aptness

In §3, we saw that two parties to a perspectival disagreement may be mired in a hermeneutic impasse. Each party appears interpretively virtuous to themselves; and indeed, they may be internally coherent. But to the other, this virtue appears to be a pernicious illusion. With luck and hard work, one or both parties may manage to "get" what they take to be the other's perspective. But there is no accessible, perspective-free standard from which to adjudicate among perspectives, to determine which is better; or indeed even to compare them, to determine how well the one has succeeded in understanding the other. Given such an impasse, should we proceed?

6.1 Strategies for Responding to Hermeneutic Impasses

One strategy, dear to philosophers since Plato, is to abjure perspectives as interpretive noise or as "cheap and dirty" heuristics for logical reasoning about the objective facts. (Contemporary proponents include Gendler 2008, Kahneman 2011, and Bloom 2016). I have argued that this is not a viable option for agents like us. We need to navigate a complex environment in real time in ways that serve our purposes. Moreover, many of our most pressing ordinary and theoretical disputes are perspectival and cannot be settled by adjudicating among finite bodies of evidence via logical principles. Even if we manage to avoid obviously perspectival tropes like metaphor and fiction, we still inevitably parse, select, connect, and respond to information in ways

46 THE VIRTUE OF OPEN-MINDEDNESS

that embody substantive assumptions about statistical distributions and normative values and priorities. In our zeal to eliminate perspectives, we risk driving them underground, confabulating rational reconstructions to justify repressed gut intuitions.

A second strategy is to cling resolutely to our existing perspectives. As Hume (1757) says, when we are "confident of the rectitude of [the] standard by which [we] judge," we should refuse to "pervert the sentiments of [our] heart" even temporarily, in contexts like fiction or political debate. While I have agreed with Hume (and Plato) that the risk of perversion is real, I have also argued that complacency poses an equally pressing, but converse, risk. The hazard of open-mindedness is a necessary condition for epistemic, moral, aesthetic, and personal growth.

A third strategy is to embrace relativism: to accept that we have no reason to think that our perspective gets things right in any metaphysically privileged sense. Its seeming right to us is a contingent historical quirk, engendered by the inevitability of our being always already thrown into some interpretive milieu. Ultimately, perspectival adequacy is a merely pragmatic matter (Nietzsche 1886; Rorty 1991; see also Elgin 2017). While this is the most epistemically humble stance, I think we must acknowledge how starkly it conflicts with our actual interpretive practices. As Hume (1757) says, it sounds plausible to say that beauty lies in the eye of the beholder, until someone asserts something as obviously wrong as that Ogilby is on a par with Milton—or that Nickelback is as good as Kendrick Lamar, that masks are repressive health hazards, or that global warming is due to natural causes.

Rather than either abjuring perspectives, clinging to prejudice, or abandoning ourselves to perspectival flux, I think we should embrace perspectives as an essential aspect of our rational agency. Perspectives are indeed inherently open-ended, intuitive, and self-effacing. In practice, they are also typically vague, inchoate, and tacit. But we can mitigate myopia and render perspectives accessible to critical assessment by actively articulating the assumptions that are encoded in their operative taxonomies and then identifying the idealizations and abstractions that those assumptions in turn presuppose.

Likewise, we do indeed inevitably operate from within a perspective and handle incoming information in a way that conforms to and tends to confirm it. But open-minded perspectival exploration, especially guided by frames, can mitigate perspectives' self-reinforcing complacency. Experiencing how compelling an alternative perspective can be from the inside, and how benighted other perspectives can appear by contrast, should induce epistemic humility in our current perspectival convictions. Humility should put us on the lookout for disconfirming evidence. And appreciating multiple, vividly engaged alternatives should push us to make an active choice among them.

6.2 Norms for Perspectival Aptness

Confronting the need to make an active choice among plausible perspectives constitutes progress over complacent myopia. However, making that choice wisely requires developing and deploying norms of perspectival aptness. A full discussion is a topic for another day; here I simply gesture at some of the relevant types of norms we should employ.

As open-ended tools for thought, perspectives cannot be directly assessed for truth. But the characterizations they generate do have contents, albeit ones that are rich, evaluatively laden, multidimensional, and holistic. We can say that a perspective is *informationally apt* to the extent that it reliably produces accurate characterizations about particular topics within its domain.

The most minimal condition on a characterization's being accurate is that the basic features it attributes to its target are actually instantiated by it. When an attributed feature f's application conditions are vague or ambiguous, the target t to which f is attributed should possess lower-level properties that locate t within f's range of permissible application. Thus, if I characterize George as overbearing, he should actually be at least somewhat more opinionated, confident, louder, and so on than other people.[8] In addition to minimal accuracy, the structure that the characterization imposes on those basic features should also be accurate. That is, features should be assigned high intensity insofar as they depart from statistically accurate baseline conditions, and also assigned high diagnosticity insofar as they are actually relevant for the agent's classificatory purposes. Features should be connected

48   THE VIRTUE OF OPEN-MINDEDNESS

to one another in ways that reflect actual patterns in the world; and the attributed grounds for those connections should actually obtain. Slightly more ambitiously, a characterization should not ignore known information that should be intense or diagnostic given the agent's statistical assumptions and values. And it should not fail to connect features that have been correlated in the agent's past experience.

In order for a perspective to *reliably* generate characterizations that are substantively and structurally accurate in these ways, it must employ a taxonomy that parses basic features into categories that actually reflect robust, stable differences in the world. It must be appropriately sensitive in updating the baseline statistical distributions that determine particular assignments of intensity and diagnosticity across contexts. And it must track contingencies that regulate changes to those distributions across times and contexts.

When these conditions are met, there is a substantive sense in which a perspectival agent is getting things epistemically right: they access, organize, and update information in ways that track objective patterns in the world. However, informational aptness is not the end of the story. For epistemic purposes, perspectives vary along multiple parameters, with competing epistemic payoffs (Flores 2021). Among other things, an agent may prioritize being opinionated over avoiding error (Fraser 2020); or achieving informational breadth over explanatory depth; or being resilient in their capacity to assimilate new information. More fundamentally, a perspective may be informationally apt but useless for an agent because it parses information into categories that are irrelevant for their practical or theoretical purposes, or that encode values they think are pernicious, such as being chaste or cute (Haslanger 2007).

A perspective is *functionally apt* if it is poised to serve the agent's purposes and values, as they prioritize among them, and in a way that generates commensurate emotional, moral, aesthetic, and/or practical responses. An agent who consistently implements a perspective that is both informationally and functionally apt is internally impervious to criticism. (In practice, of course, such agents are exceedingly rare.) There is no evidence that an interlocutor can provide to them about conflicts among their substantive assumptions and values or between those assumptions and reality that would rationally compel them to alter their perspective.

However, as we have seen, that interlocutor may still rationally disagree with them if they reject their taxonomy, values, and/or priorities. What should we make of persistent disagreement among even perspectivally ideal agents?

Some such cases of disagreement invite ecumenical relativism. For instance, one aesthete may grant that a painting is serene and profound but prefer another because it is more energetic and disorienting. Similarly, a structural engineer may grant that a theoretical physicist's theory is more elegant, encompassing, and accurate but prefer their own theory because they prioritize predicting the evolving properties of middle-sized dry goods. However, many candidates for perspectival diversity are more difficult to accept, because they are grounded in irreconcilable clashes of value. In these cases, sincere articulation and assessment can help to pinpoint the grounds of disagreement and perhaps foster appreciation for the other perspective's informational and functional aptness. However, this is unlikely to break a hermeneutic impasse or to produce perspectival conversion, on the assumption that each perspective has achieved its own internal harmony.

7 Amelioration

Applying norms of the sort I gestured at in §6.2 can help us to diagnose others' perspectival limitations and our own inconsistencies, and illuminate potential paths for addressing both. This work is important and ongoing. Nevertheless, the more fundamental question remains: how do we flourish as perspectival agents while navigating the twin risks of complacency and perversion? The deep problem with perspectives is not that they are selective and preferential. That much is an inevitable consequence of being finite cognitive agents. Nor is the problem even that perspectives are self-effacing and self-reinforcing. If we are lucky enough to inhabit a perspective that is informationally and functionally apt for its environment, then it will work well even if we can't discern or validate its operative principles. Even myopia isn't so bad, if we are flexible enough to address blind spots as they arise. Rather, the deep problem is complacency and the risk that our perspectives

50 THE VIRTUE OF OPEN-MINDEDNESS

stagnate and ossify in ways that prevent us from shifting gears when our environment changes in ways that undermine functional aptness.

As I have emphasized, there is no sure-fire recipe for avoiding complacency or perversion. Instead, I propose three broad strategies for honing our interpretive skills without abandoning our perspectival compass. Unfortunately, none are particularly revolutionary or sure-fire; but they can still be helpful.

First, we should cultivate perspectival habits that are flexible but also resilient. Given the risk of perversion, we should mostly gather information from sources we take to be reliable; we should spend most of our time with people, news sources, and art we find congenial. When we notice gaps between our reflective principles and our intuitive inclinations, we should deploy corrective frames to bring the latter into line. But we should also make regular forays into alternative milieus, in sufficient empathetic depth to implement their operative perspectival dispositions. Different degrees and directions of departure will fall beyond the pale for different agents. Perspectival play requires time, motivation, mental space, and imaginative flexibility. Some people lack these resources; for others, the risk of perversion may be too great. In particular, greater social power plausibly imposes a greater obligation to explore. Still, we should all strive for a modicum of sincere perspectival curiosity. After a perspectival venture, we should not simply perpetuate the perspectival habits we now find most comfortable. Rather, we should interrogate our current inclinations and commitments—on our own, but especially in dialogue with those we trust (Dover 2022). We should actually ask Nehamas's questions: Who am I? By what standards should I evaluate myself?

Second, in answering these questions, we should embrace logic—not as a retreat from perspectives, but as a complementary tool. Most intuitive perspectives function to integrate us into contexts so that we can process and respond to local information in real time in ways that reflect our currently prioritized values and purposes. By contrast, logic is a tool for achieving cross-contextual consistency: for combining and processing stable information according to general rules in ways that track truth and other values (Camp 2015). Indeed, logic is itself a perspective: a disposition to interpret information in terms of contextually stable, formally individuated, truth-tracking rules. We can use logic to stabilize and revise our more worldly perspectives by explicating the contents of our particular characterizations, our global assumptions about statistical distributions and explanatory connections, and our practical, theoretical, and evaluative commitments. Here, it is worth noting that logic can take many forms: not just predicate calculi, but also diagrams (Shin 1994), graphs (Pearl 2000), and maps (Camp 2018), some of which may more perspicuously reflect the functionally operative structures of our perspectives and their resulting characterizations. And here too, while logical articulation and assessment can be conducted alone, they are often most fruitfully engaged in conversation.

Finally, we should beware the siren song of simplicity. Perspectival frames are cognitively and communicatively useful because they compress complex, multi-dimensional perspectives into more schematic, stable, shareable principles. This is especially important at the beginning of inquiry, when we are groping through unfamiliar territory. But the world we care about is often too messy and our values too nuanced to be adequately captured by catchy slogans. Thus, as theoretical inquiry and practical engagement proceed, we should seek to avoid ossifying our thinking into rigid, blinkered structures, and expect catchy slogans to give way to multi-dimensional, multi-layered theories (Camp 2020; Camp and Flores 2024).

There is no sure sign of perspectival aptness. Each of us is undoubtedly myopic, confused, and complacent every day. Sometimes we catch ourselves; sometimes others call us out. Often that is annoying; sometimes it is mean or misplaced. Still, we should try to hear and learn from each other, especially when we are most confident in our interpretive rectitude.

Notes

1. Thanks to audiences at Brown University, Institut Jean Nicod, Cornell University, Sheffield University, the University of Pennsylvania, Uppsala University, and the 2020 Central APA, as well as participants in my 2019 Rutgers University seminar in aesthetics, Susanna Siegel's 2020 Harvard University seminar in epistemology, and Georgi Gardiner's 2021 University of Tennessee seminar in epistemology. Special thanks to Antony Aumann, Tez Clark, Carolina Flores, Deborah Marber, Thi Nguyen, and Joy Shim for extensive comments and feedback. Thanks to Stephen Laurence for the rendition of Figure 1.

52   THE VIRTUE OF OPEN-MINDEDNESS

2. The last several years have seen an explosion of philosophical interest in the empirical basis, theoretical analysis, and normative implications of attention; see especially Wu (2023), Siegel (2017), Munton (2021), Watzl (2021), and Whiteley (2022).
3. For Rosch (1976), "basic" categories are categorical kinds like DOG, as distinguished from subordinate categories like SPANIEL and superordinate categories like ANIMAL. As I am using the term, basic features are the primary terms in which an agent cognizes a domain. For someone invested in dog breeds, SPANIEL might be a basic feature. I distinguish basic features from the lower-level features that determine the extensions of basic features, and from higher-level structural features like prominence and centrality.
4. Thus, a 2008 Pew study found that 51% of evangelical Christians believe that belief in religions other than Christianity can lead to eternal life, and 26% allow that atheists can achieve salvation; while according to a 2011 Pew survey, 95% of evangelical Christian leaders say that these beliefs are incompatible with being an evangelical Christian.
5. One popular strategy for cashing out the difference between believing and intuitively "getting" is to construe beliefs as reflective, abstract, reason-responsive attitudes, in contrast to a primordial system of automatic, embodied, associative cognition (e.g., Kahnemann 2011; Gendler 2008, 2011; Frankish 2010). While "dual systems" theorists rightly draw attention to how much of our cognitive lives is driven by intuition and its departures from reflective judgment, a dualist approach imposes a cleaner and deeper cleavage between intuition and reflection than is warranted. First, the various criteria that supposedly differentiate the two "systems" are a matter of degree and frequently diverge (e.g., Bargh 1994; Carruthers 2014; Mandelbaum 2016). Second, we deploy perspectives on sophisticated, abstract domains like science as much as on deeply enculturated domains like food and gender. In neither case is intuition impervious to reflection. Interpretive disputes in both everyday life and theoretical discourse often involve articulating and debating about perspectival assumptions; and often enough, we modulate our intuitive thinking at least temporarily in response to others' arguments.
6. At least for in-group assessments of independently identifiable 'core' stereotypic features for gender and race/ethnicity (though notably, not for nationality or political affiliation; Jussim et al. 2015).
7. For simplicity, I have focused on perspectivally divergent agents encountering a common body of information. The risks of myopia and complacency are exacerbated by the fact that perspectives affect which sources and types of information agents encounter and trust (Nguyen 2018).
8. When the attribution is generic—say, I characterize snakes as dangerous or women as cooperative—then the corresponding generic should be true, where this may not require a high degree of correlation.

Works Cited

Anderson, Craig, Mark Lepper, and Lee Ross. 1980. "Perseverance of Social Theories: The Role of Explanation in the Persistence of Discredited Information." *Journal of Personality and Social Psychology* 39(6): 1037.

Bargh, John. 1994. "The Four Horsemen of Automaticity: Awareness, Intention, Efficiency, and Control in Social Cognition." In *Handbook of Social Cognition*, vol. 1, *Basic Processes*, 2nd ed., ed. R. S. Wyer Jr. and T. K. Srull (pp. 1–40). Mahwah, NJ: Lawrence Erlbaum.

Begby, Endre. 2013. "The Epistemology of Prejudice." *Thought* 2: 90–99.

Boyd, Richard. 1999. "Homeostasis, Species, and Higher Taxa." In *Species: New Interdisciplinary Essays*, ed. Robert Wilson (141–185). Cambridge: MIT Press.

PERSPECTIVAL COMPLACENCY, PERVERSION 53

Brownstein, Michael. 2016. "Context and the Ethics of Implicit Bias." *Implicit Bias and Philosophy*, vol. 2, ed. J. Saul and M. Brownstein. Oxford: Oxford University Press, 215–234.

Camp, Elisabeth. 2006. "Metaphor and That Certain 'Je Ne Sais Quoi.'" *Philosophical Studies* 129(1): 1–25.

Camp, Elisabeth. 2008. "Showing, Telling, and Seeing: Metaphor and 'Poetic' Language." *Baltic International Yearbook of Cognition, Logic, and Communication*, vol. 3, *A Figure of Speech: Metaphor,* 1–24. Manhattan, KS: New Prairie Press.

Camp, Elisabeth. 2009. "'Two Varieties of Literary Imagination: Metaphor, Fiction, and Thought Experiments." *Midwest Studies in Philosophy* 33(1): 107–130.

Camp, Elisabeth. 2013. "Slurring Perspectives." *Analytic Philosophy* 54(3): 330–349.

Camp, Elisabeth. 2015. "Logical Concepts and Associative Characterizations." In *The Conceptual Mind: New Directions in the Study of Concepts*, ed. E. Margolis and S. Laurence (591–621). Cambridge, MA: MIT Press.

Camp, Elisabeth. 2017a. "Perspectives in Imaginative Engagement with Fiction,. *Philosophical Perspectives: Philosophy of Mind,* ed. J. Hawthorne, 31(1): 73–102.

Camp, Elisabeth. 2017b. "Why Metaphors Make Good Insults: Perspectives, Presupposition, and Pragmatics." *Philosophical Studies* 174(1): 47–64.

Camp, Elisabeth. 2018. "Why Maps Are Not Propositional." In *Non-Propositional Intentionality*, ed. A. Grzankowski and M. Montague 19–45 Oxford: Oxford University Press.

Camp, Elisabeth. 2019. "Perspectives and Frames in Pursuit of Ultimate Understanding." In *Varieties of Understanding: New Perspectives from Philosophy, Psychology, and Theology*, ed. Stephen Grimm (17–45). Oxford: Oxford University Press.

Camp, Elisabeth. 2020. "Imaginative Frames for Scientific Inquiry: Metaphors, Telling Facts, and Just-So Stories." In *The Scientific Imagination*, ed. P. Godfrey-Smith and A. Levy (304–336). Oxford: Oxford University Press.

Camp, Elisabeth. 2023. "Agency, Stability, and Permeability in 'Games'": Commentary on Thi Nguyen's 'Games and the Art of Agency.'" *Journal of Ethics and Social Philosophy* 23(3): 448–462.

Camp, Elisabeth and Carolina Flores. 2024. "Playing with Labels: Identity Terms as Tools for Building Agency." *Philosophical Quarterly* 74(4):1103–1136.

Carnap, Rudolf. 1928/1967. *The Logical Structure of the World*, trans. Rolf A. George. Berkeley: University of California Press.

Carruthers, Peter. 2014. "The Fragmentation of Reasoning." In *Cognición social y lenguaje: La intersubjetividad en la evolución de la especie y en el desarrollo del niño*, ed. Pablo Quintanilla, Carla Mantilla, and Paola Cépeda. Lima: Pontificia Universidad Católica del Perú.

Clavel Vázquez, María Jimena and Adriana Clavel-Vázquez. 2023. "Robustly Embodied Imagination and the Limits of Perspective-Taking." *Philosophical Studies* 180(4): 1395–1420.

Currie, Gregory. 1997. "The Paradox of Caring: Fiction and the Philosophy of Mind." In *Emotion and the Arts*, ed. H. Mette and S. Laver. New York: Oxford University Press.

Dover, Daniela. 2022. "The Conversational Self." *Mind* 131(521): 193–230.

54 THE VIRTUE OF OPEN-MINDEDNESS

Du Bois, W. E. B. 1903. *The Souls of Black Folk.* Chicago: A. C. McClurg.

Duncan, Birt L. 1976. "Differential Social Perception and Attribution of Intergroup Violence: Testing the Lower Limits of Stereotyping of Blacks." *Journal of Personality and Social Psychology* 34: 590–598.

Eckert, Penelope. 2000. *Language Variation as Social Practice: The Linguistic Construction of Identity in Belten High.* New York: Wiley-Blackwell.

Finnegan, Eimear, Jane Oakhill, and Alan Garnham. 2015. "Counter-stereotypical Pictures as a Strategy for Overcoming Spontaneous Gender Stereotypes." *Frontiers in Psychology* 6: 1291.

Flores, Carolina. 2021. "Epistemic Styles." *Philosophical Topics* 49(2): 35–55.

Fraser, Rachel. 2020. "Epistemic FOMO." *The Cambridge Humanities Review* 16 [online]. https://cambridgereview.cargo.site/Dr-Rachel-Fraser.

Gawronski, B. and Cesario, J. 2013. "Of Mice and Men: What Animal Research Can Tell Us about Context Effects on Automatic Response in Humans." *Personality and Social Psychology Review* 17(2): 187–215.

Gelman, Susan. 2005. "Essentialism in Everyday Thought." *Psychological Science Agenda* 19(5): 1–6.

Gendler, Tamar Szabó. 2008. "Alief and Belief." *Journal of Philosophy* 105(10): 634–663.

Gendler, Tamar Szabó. 2011. "On the Epistemic Costs of Implicit Bias." *Philosophical Studies* 156: 33–63.

Gibson, J. J. 1979. *The Ecological Approach to Visual Perception.* New York: Houghton, Mifflin.

Goldman, Alvin. 1992. "Empathy, Mind, and Morals." *Proceedings and Addresses of the American Philosophical Association* 66(3): 17–41.

Hacking, Ian. 1995. "The Looping Effect of Human Kinds." In *Causal Cognition: A Multidisciplinary Debate*, ed. D. Sperber, D. Premack, and A. J. Premack (351–394). Oxford: Clarendon Press,

Haidt, Jonathan and Craig Joseph. 2004. "Intuitive Ethics: How Innately Prepared Intuitions Generate Culturally Variable Virtues." *Daedalus* 133(4): 55–66.

Haslam, Nick and Rothschild, Louis. 2000. "Essentialist Beliefs about Social Categories." *British Journal of Social Psychology* 39(1): 113–127.

Haslanger, Sally. 2007. " 'But Mom, Crop-Tops Are Cute!' Social Knowledge, Social Structure and Ideology Critique." *Philosophical Issues* 17: *The Metaphysics of Epistemology*, 70–91.

Haslanger, Sally. 2015. "Social Structure, Narrative and Explanation." *Canadian Journal of Philosophy* 45(1): 1–15.

hooks, bell. 1992. "Eating the Other: Desire and Resistance." In *Black Looks: Race and Representation.* Boston: South End Press, 21–39.

Hume, David. 1757/1985. "On the Standard of Taste." Reprinted in *Essays: Moral, Political and Legal*, ed. E. Miller (227–249). Indianapolis: Liberty Fund.

Judd, Charles and Bernadette Park. 1993. "Definition and Assessment of Accuracy in Social Stereotypes." *Psychological Review* 100(1): 109–128.

Jussim, Lee, Jarret T. Crawford, and Rachel S. Rubinstein. 2015. "Stereotype (In) accuracy in Perceptions of Groups and Individuals." *Current Directions in Psychological Science* 24(6): 490–497.

Kahneman, Daniel. 2011. *Thinking Fast and Slow.* New York: Farrar, Straus and Giroux.

PERSPECTIVAL COMPLACENCY, PERVERSION   55

Kuhn, Thomas. 1962. *The Structure of Scientific Revolutions*. Chicago: Chicago University Press.

Langton, Rae. 2019. "Blocking as Counterspeech." In *New Work on Speech Acts*, ed. D. Fogal, D. Harris, and M. Moss. Oxford: Oxford University Press, 144–162.

Leslie, Sarah Jane. 2008. "Generics: Cognition and acquisition." *Philosophical Review* 117(1): 1–47.

Leslie, Sarah Jane. 2014. "Carving Up the Social World with Generics." *Oxford Studies in Experimental Philosophy* 1: 208–232.

Lewis, David. 1979. "Scorekeeping in a Language Game." *Journal of Philosophical Logic* 8: 339–359.

Longino, Helen and Doell, D. 1983. "Body, Bias, and Behavior: A Comparative Analysis of Reasoning in Two Areas of Biological Science." *Signs* 9: 206–227.

Lord, Charles, Lee Ross, and Mark Lepper. 1979. "Biased Assimilation and Attitude Polarization: The Effects of Prior Theories on Subsequently Considered Evidence," *Journal of Personality and Social Psychology* 37:2098–2109.

Lord, Charles and Cheryl Taylor. 2009. "Biased Assimilation: Effects of Assumptions and Expectations on the Interpretation of New Evidence." *Social and Personality Psychology Compass* 3(5): 827–841.

Lugones, María. 1987. "Playfulness, 'World'-Travelling, and Loving Perception." *Hypatia* 2(2): 3–19.

Mandelbaum, Eric. 2016. "Attitude, Inference, Association: On the Propositional Structure of Implicit Bias." *Noûs* 50(3): 629–658.

Mathis, Klaus and Ariel David Steffen. 2015. "From Rational Choice to Behavioural Economics: Theoretical Foundations, Empirical Findings and Legal Implications." In *European Perspectives on Behavioural Law and Economics*, ed. K. Mathis (31–48). London: Springer.

McClelland, Tom and Paulina Sliwa. 2023. "Gendered Affordance Perception and Unequal Domestic Labour," *Philosophy and Phenomenological Research* 107(2): 501–524.

McDowell, John. 1981. "Non-Cognitivism and Rule-Following." In *Wittgenstein: To Follow a Rule*, ed. S. Holtzman and C. Leich (141–172). London: Routledge and Kegan Paul.

Moreno, Kristen and Galen Bodenhausen. 1999. "Resisting Stereotype Change: The Role of Motivation and Attentional Capacity in Defending Social Beliefs." *Group Processes & Intergroup Relations* 2(1): 5–16.

Morton, Jennifer. 2014. "Cultural Code-Switching: Straddling the Achievement Gap." *Journal of Political Philosophy* 22(3): 259–281.

Munton, Jessie. 2021. "Prejudice as the Misattribution of Salience." *Analytic Philosophy* 64(1):1–19.

Murphy, Gregory and Doug Medin. 1985. "The Role of Theories in Conceptual Coherence," *Psychological Review* 92: 289–316.

Nehamas, Alexander. 2000. "An Essay on Beauty and Judgment." *Threepenny Review* [online].

Nickerson, Raymond. 1998. "Confirmation Bias: A Ubiquitous Phenomenon in Many Guises." *Review of General Psychology* 2(2): 175–220.

Nietszche, Friedrich. 1886/1966. *Beyond Good and Evil*, trans. Walter Kaufmann. New York: Vintage.

Nguyen, C. Thi. 2018. "Echo Chambers and Epistemic Bubbles." *Episteme* 1–21.

Nguyen, C. Thi. 2020. *Games: Agency as Art*. Oxford: Oxford University Press.

Nguyen, C. Thi. 2021. "The Seductions of Clarity." *Royal Institute of Philosophy. Supplement* 89:227–255.

Pavlov, P. Ivan. 1927. "Conditioned Reflexes: An Investigation of the Physiological Activity of the Cerebral Cortex." *Nature* 121(3052): 662–664.

Pearl, Judea. 2000. *Causality*. Cambridge: Cambridge University Press.

Proust, Marcel. 1913. *In Search of Lost Time*, trans. C. K. Scott Moncrieff, ed. William C. Carter. New Haven: Yale University Press.

Rorty, Richard. 1991. *Objectivity, Relativism, and Truth: Philosophical Papers*, vol. 1. Cambridge: Cambridge University Press.

Rosch, Eleanor. 1976. "Principles of Classification." In *Cognition and Categorization*, ed. E. Rosch and B. Lloyd (27–48). Hillsdale, NJ: Lawrence Erlbaum.

Ryan, Carey, Charles Judd, and Bernadette Park. 1996. "Effects of Racial Stereotypes on Judgments of Individuals: The Moderating Role of Perceived Group Variability." *Journal of Experimental Social Psychology* 32(1): 91–103.

Schmader, Toni, Michael Johns, and Chad Forbes. 2008. "An Integrated Process Model of Stereotype Threat Effects on Performance." *Psychological Review* 115(2): 336–356.

Siegel, Susanna. 2017. *The Rationality of Perception*. Oxford: Oxford University Press.

Simons, D. J., and Chabris, C. F. 1999. "Gorillas in Our Midst: Sustained Inattentional Blindness for Dynamic Events." *Perception* 28(9): 1059–1074.

Shin, Sun-Joo. 1994. *The Logical Status of Diagrams*. Cambridge: Cambridge University Press.

Sloman, Steven, Bradley Love, and Woo-Kyoung Ahn. 1998. "Feature Centrality and Conceptual Coherence." *Cognitive Science* 22(2): 189–228.

Small, Deborah, Jennifer Lerner, and Baruch Fischhoff. 2006. "Emotion Priming and Attributions for Terrorism: Americans' Reactions in a National Field Experiment." *Political Psychology* 27(2): 289–298.

Smith, Zadie, 2019. "Fascinated to Presume: In Defense of Fiction." *The New York Review of Books*. https://www.nybooks.com/articles/2019/10/24/zadie-smith-in-defense-of-fiction/.

Stalnaker, Robert. 2014. *Context*. Oxford: Oxford University Press.

Steele, Claude. 2010. *Whistling Vivaldi: How Stereotypes Affect Us and What We Can Do*. New York: Norton.

Thagard, Paul. 1989. "Explanatory Coherence." *Behavioral and Brain Sciences* 12: 435– 502.

Trout, J. D. 2002. "Scientific Explanation and the Sense of Understanding." *Philosophy of Science* 69: 212–233.

Tversky, Amos. 1977. "Features of Similarity." *Psychological Review* 84: 327–352.

Watzl, Sebastian. 2017. *Structuring Mind. The Nature of Attention and How It Shapes Consciousness*. Oxford: Oxford University Press.

Whiteley, Ella. 2022. "Harmful Salience Perspectives. In *Salience: A Philosophical Inquiry*, ed. Sophie Archer. New York: Routledge.

Williams, Bernard. 1985. *Ethics and the Limits of Philosophy*. Cambridge, MA: Harvard University Press.

Wittgenstein, Ludwig. 1953. *Philosophical Investigations*, trans. G. E. M. Anscombe. Oxford: Basil Blackwell.

Wu, Wayne. 2023. "On Attention and Norms: An Opinionated Review of Recent Work." *Analysis*, anad056, https://doi.org/10.1093/analys/anad056.

Young, Iris Marion. 1997. "Asymmetrical Reciprocity: On Moral Respect, Wonder, and Enlarged Thought." In *Intersecting Voices: Dilemmas of Gender, Political Philosophy, and Policy*. Princeton, NJ: Princeton University Press.

2

Perspective-Taking and a Flexible Mind: A Tibetan Buddhist Approach to Open-Mindedness

Emily McRae

If we think about open-mindedness (OM), as Jason Baehr does, as the willingness and ability to "transcend a default cognitive standpoint in order to take up or take seriously the merits of a distinct cognitive standpoint," then it is not an exaggeration to say that Indo-Tibetan Buddhist philosophy is centrally concerned with OM (Baehr 2011, 202). Indo-Tibetan Buddhist traditions do not theorize OM as a distinct virtue but tend to think of the transcendence of default perspectives as an epistemic and moral skill, or set of skills, that is required for moral cultivation, including the development of love and compassion, and for the cultivation of wisdom. In this chapter, I aim to introduce two moral-epistemic skills of the Indo-Tibetan Buddhist tradition that are closely related to Western philosophical conceptions of OM, pliancy (Sanskrit: *praśrabdhi*; Tibetan: *shin sbyang*) and perspective-taking ("exchanging self and other," Tibetan: *bdag gzhan brje ba*).

I argue that thinking about OM through the lens of these Buddhist moral-epistemic skills highlights dimensions of OM that have been under-theorized in contemporary Western literature, namely, (i) the moral dimensions, (ii) the embodied or physical dimensions, and (iii) the affective dimensions. I argue that OM is not simply about transcending default cognitive perspectives but affective ones as well, and one of the main benefits of OM and pliancy is an affective moral sensitivity and freedom from morally problematic affective states.

Emily McRae, *Perspective-Taking and a Flexible Mind: A Tibetan Buddhist Approach to Open-Mindedness* In: *The Virtue of Open-Mindedness and Perspective.* Edited by: Wayne D. Riggs, Oxford University Press. © Oxford University Press 2025.
DOI: 10.1093/9780190080723.003.0003

I then turn to Indo-Tibetan practices of perspective-taking, which many Buddhist philosophers offer as exercises for transcending our default cognitive and affective standpoints. I argue that perspective-taking is an important part of cultivating OM and defend perspective-taking as an ethical practice from some recent objections (Friedman 1993; Maibom 2013).

1 Pliancy (praśrabdhi, shin tu sbyang ba)

In contemporary Western accounts, such as Baehr's, OM is generally conceived of as an epistemic virtue (Adler 2004; Baehr 2011; Hare 2006; Kwong 2016; Riggs 2010).[1] It is the intellectual excellence associated with the ability to take up new cognitive perspectives—often, but not always, perspectives that challenge one's default perspective—in service of a greater understanding of truth.[2] It opposes, most fundamentally, a rigidity of thinking, which can manifest as narrow-mindedness and dogmatism. Of course, everyone has the ability to take up a new cognitive perspective—this is part of learning—but a person with the epistemic virtue of OM excels at the consideration of novel standpoints, often illustrated in cases where the new standpoint is radically foreign or when one is particularly invested in one's default perspective. A typical example from this literature is the scientist who seriously considers an unconventional hypothesis—one that ends up greatly advancing scientific knowledge—despite ridicule from disbelieving colleagues (for example, Baehr 2011, 193, and Arpaly 2011, 81).

The Buddhist Abhidharma tradition discusses a mental quality that at least partially tracks this contemporary Western understanding of OM: pliancy (Sanskrit: *praśrabdhi*, Tibetan: *shin sbyang*; also translated as flexibility and, in some cases, serenity).[3] Definitions of pliancy tend to focus on the ability to be flexible, a quality that is applicable to both the body and the mind. The fourth-century Buddhist scholar Asanga defines pliancy as "the maneuverability of the body and mind acquired by relaxing the rigidity of the body and mind" (2001, 10). According to another great fourth-century philosopher (and Asanga's half-brother) Vasubandhu, pliancy is the property of the mind "through which thought is made clever, i.e., light or apt or

60   THE VIRTUE OF OPEN-MINDEDNESS

versatile" (2012, 516). A pliant mind is one that is flexible and versatile enough to engage an object of cognition without resistance or rigidity.

Pliancy is not itself (what Western ethicists might consider) a full-fledged virtue. Buddhist thinkers categorize it as a wholesome (Sanskrit: *kusala*) mental factor—one of eleven—that is present in any virtuous mental state.[4] Whenever we experience a virtuous mental state, such as a generous thought, we are making use of a basic pliancy, a basic maneuverability of mind. Without pliancy we simply could not direct our mind to a virtuous object; the mind must be flexible enough to engage in virtuous mental activity, especially virtuous thought that challenges a deeply ingrained habit of mind, such as self-centeredness. Buddhist thinkers compare this basic moral skill of pliancy—"mere pliancy"—with its more advanced form, "special pliancy." Like Asanga and Vasubandhu, the 20th-century Tibetan Buddhist philosopher Denma Lochö Rinpoche defines the basic form of pliancy as "that which provides serviceability such that the mind can be directed to a virtuous object." Special pliancy, however, is "a case of serviceability such that the mind can be directed to any virtuous object as much as one likes" (Zahler 2009, 165). Special pliancy is an excellence that is usually discussed in the context of practicing calm abiding (Tibetan: *zhi gnas*) meditation. Although it is conceived in the context of meditative concentration, special pliancy, like mere pliancy, is not a skill of concentration; it is the skill of being mentally flexible enough to take up an object in order to concentrate on it. What makes it "special" is the fact that the object can be taken up by the mind for as long as one chooses.

Like OM, pliancy is understood in Buddhist philosophy in opposition to the rigid thinking and inflexible mental habits that prevent a more accurate understanding of the world. It also shares with OM the quality of acting as an antidote to laziness. Baehr argues that OM is not only opposed to the vices of "narrow-mindedness, close-mindedness, dogmatism, prejudice, and bias" but also the vices of "intellectual hastiness, impatience, and laziness" that lead one to make "hasty or premature conclusions" (Baehr 2011, 195). Laziness is a kind of rigidity, a resistance to changing a habit. Pliancy is also seen as that which opposes laziness, since on the Buddhist view laziness is a kind of reduced serviceability of the mind; the lazy, hasty mind

PERSPECTIVE-TAKING AND A FLEXIBLE MIND   61

lacks the maneuverability of the pliant mind and so cannot be reliably directed to a virtuous object (Lati Rinpoche, et al 1997, 53–56; Zahler 2009, 141).

Pliancy, then, shares with OM two important features. Both are characterized by the skill of cognitive flexibility and both are opposed to vices related to mental rigidity, which includes a broad range of faults (from dogmatism, to prejudice, to laziness). But, unlike many accounts of OM in contemporary Western philosophy, discussions of pliancy in the Buddhist philosophy tend to highlight (i) the moral dimensions of pliancy, (ii) the physical component of pliancy, and (iii) the ways that pliancy relates to our emotional lives. In what follows, I argue that conceptions of OM could benefit from taking seriously these three dimensions.

1.1 The Moral Dimensions of Pliancy and OM

That pliancy is a moral quality is clear from its basic categorization as one of the virtuous or wholesome qualities of mind. This is the first moral dimension of pliancy: it is employed in virtuous thought and is therefore a kind of prerequisite or basic component of virtuous mental activity. But sometimes the moral significance of pliancy is more direct. The early 20th-century Tibetan philosopher Mipham Rinpoche defines pliancy as "the ability to apply body and mind to virtue (*dge ba*). Its function is to overcome negative tendencies" (24). Here, pliancy is not simply the lack of mental rigidity that allows virtuous mental activity to occur but is defined in terms of virtue—the pliant mind is one that can be applied to virtue. Defining pliancy in this way rules out the problematic cases of making one's mind flexible for the sake of taking up vicious mental activity. The mind can surely do such a thing, but it would not be considered pliancy on Mipham Rinpoche's account. This marks the second moral dimension of pliancy: morality sets the boundaries of, or limiting conditions for, pliancy. Pliancy is applicable only in the context of virtue or the cultivation of virtue. This suggests, in addition to narrow-mindedness, rigidity, dogmatism, and laziness, pliancy is also opposed to non-moral mental flexibility, that is, the vice of being open to hateful or vicious mental activities.

62   THE VIRTUE OF OPEN-MINDEDNESS

The third moral dimension of pliancy relates to the "negative tendencies" that is pliancy is said to overcome (in Mipham Rinpoche's definition). The late 20th-century Tibetan thinker Geshe Lodrö defines these "negative tendencies" as "that which causes the yogic practitioner to dislike aiming the mind at an object of observation" (Powers 1995, 79). The function of pliancy is to overcome the dislike we may feel when we focus our minds on oppositional or difficult objects, as being able to focus on difficult objects is sometimes necessary for virtuous mental activity. We may, for example, be averse to considering the ways we are contributing to a conflict, or we may dislike focusing our minds on injustices in which we are complicit. For Buddhist ethicists, this dislike can be explained in moral terms: the reason we dislike taking up a virtuous perspective is because it challenges a default non-virtuous perspective, such as self-centeredness, resentment, or spite. Being able to overcome aversion to morality is an important, but sometimes overlooked, skill of ethical life. It is what gives us the cognitive and affective freedom to engage in virtuous ways of thinking and acting, which supports our development as moral agents. When we cannot direct our minds toward uncomfortable or unfamiliar objects, we are not able to learn and grow morally. The third moral dimension of pliancy, then, is that it makes possible moral growth.

These three moral dimensions of pliancy also apply to OM. As I have argued in a previous article, it is important to understand OM not only as an epistemic virtue but also a moral one, since there are moral reasons to be open-minded (McRae 2016). We are sometimes motivated to be open-minded not from the commitment to understand the truth but from the desire to care for someone more effectively. (This desire need not be in conflict with the desire to understand the truth; on the contrary, it is likely that understanding the truth will support effective caring, but here the moral, rather than intellectual, desire is primary.) Looking at the moral contours of pliancy is helpful for understanding open-mindedness since OM shares with pliancy all three moral dimensions. First, at least some level of OM is necessary for virtuous mental activity for the reasons given by Buddhist Abhidharma thinkers: the ability to take up new perspectives is a basic prerequisite for a host of virtuous mental activities, such as the empathic understanding of others' testimony, the anticipation of others'

PERSPECTIVE-TAKING AND A FLEXIBLE MIND   63

needs, and deflation of one's own self-centeredness. There is a "mere OM" that is required for basic moral function.

The second moral dimension of pliancy—that moral concerns set the conceptual boundaries of pliancy—is also applicable to open-mindedness. For OM to make sense as a virtue of any kind there must be normative limitations on the range of types of cases that count as OM in order to avoid obvious counterexamples. In the context of epistemic virtue, OM should not include having a mind so open that "your brains fall out" (Baehr 2011, 192). Open-mindedness as an epistemic virtue needs to be moored to furthering the goal of understanding of truth in order to distinguish it from a flighty, superficial curiosity and other forms of non-discerning cognitive engagement. In the context of moral virtue, OM needs to be defined in terms of a moral good—I suggest the care and respect for members of the moral community as the main moral good—in order to distinguish it from the skill of easily taking up novel, hateful perspectives. This skill is not a virtue because it is neither contained nor informed by the moral commitment to care and respect. President Trump's recent (2017) claim that there are "good people" on both sides of the conflict between white supremacists and anti-racist activists in Charlottesville, Virginia, for example, is not open-minded on this account, but (at best) morally non-discerning.

On the Buddhist view, pliancy functions as a way to overcome morally negative tendencies, particularly aversion to engaging certain virtuous mental objects or perspectives. I have argued previously that aversion to taking up alternative perspectives, as well as clinging to default perspectives, is a major barrier to the cultivation and application of open-mindedness as a moral virtue (McRae 2016). But what the Indo-Tibetan Buddhist discussions of pliancy suggest is that not only do the negative mental tendencies of craving and aversion frustrate the mind's ability to take up novel perspectives but that the cultivation of pliancy (and, I submit, OM) is itself also a way to lessen the hold of such tendencies. This explanation highlights the need to understand the *cultivation* of OM as moral virtue—how it is developed and what happens when it is developed. I discuss perspective-taking as a potentially effective tool for cultivating OM in section 2 of this chapter ("Perspective-Taking and Transcending Default Standpoints").

64　THE VIRTUE OF OPEN-MINDEDNESS

1.2　Embodied OM? The Physical Dimensions of Pliancy

One aspect of the Buddhist definitions of pliancy that might stand out to a reader situated in the Western philosophical traditions is their constant inclusion of physical pliancy, or pliancy of body, in broader discussions of pliancy. Physical pliancy, according to some Tibetan commentators, is what makes the body flexible, resilient, and able to overcome fatigue. It "removes physical tiredness," which allows one to use the body "for whatever virtuous purpose one wishes, without any sense of hardship" and makes that body feel "as light as cotton" (Zahler 2009, 167; see also Lodrö 1998, 100). The inclusion of the pliancy of the body marks a clear point of departure from Western philosophical discussions of open-mindedness, according to which it is the mind, not the body, that is open. To complicate matters further, the Buddhist philosophers are not simply claiming that there is virtue in pliancy of the body, but that this bodily pliancy is (somehow) similar to mental pliancy and that the presence of physical pliancy is (somehow) related to the presence of mental pliancy.

These claims might seem prima facie implausible. What does having a flexible body have to do with having an open and pliant mind? Surely, we could have one without the other. And why even bother to include discussions of bodily pliancy at all if it is mental pliancy that really matters, morally and epistemically? It may be helpful to note that the inclusion of the pliancy of the body is also problematized in the Buddhist texts quoted earlier. Vasubandhu, for example, presents a debate between different early Buddhist schools on how to justify physical pliancy as "a member of enlightenment" since the body isn't the right kind of thing to become enlightened (516–517). Vasubandhu's final answer, it seems, is that the pliancy of the body should be included in our general understanding of pliancy because it is a "favorable condition" for the cultivation of mental pliancy (517).

I interpret Vasubandhu as making the fairly weak claim that having a pliant body (that is, a body that you can apply to virtuous activity) tends to support the cultivation of having a pliant mind (that is, a mind that you can apply to virtuous activity). I don't think he is making, or should make, the stronger claim that pliancy of the body is a necessary condition of mental pliancy, since there are clear counterexamples to

PERSPECTIVE-TAKING AND A FLEXIBLE MIND 65

this claim: there are people who have wonderfully pliant minds yet do not have bodies that are especially pliant (for instance, Stephen Hawking).[5] Having a pliant body is simply a support for having pliant mind; it can help, but certainly is not necessary for, the cultivation of mental pliancy. It is important to remember that the pliancy of the body refers to the serviceability of the body, whether the body can serve as a vehicle for virtuous action. Assuming that there are many ways for a body to apply itself to virtue, physical pliancy, presumably, can take many forms. (Physical pliancy is not, for example, tracking contemporary ideals of physical fitness or ability versus disability.) So, when you are able to use your body for virtuous activity—however that manifests—you are creating a supportive environment for cultivating mental pliancy.

It is not clear to me how Vasubandhu—or other Buddhist Abhidharma scholars—understood the scope or depth of this claim. There is a trivial interpretation of his claim: physical pliancy is a "favorable condition" of mental pliancy simply because it is a favorable condition for doing anything virtuous. All other things being equal, it is helpful (but not necessary) for moral life to have a body one can apply to virtue. This interpretation is trivial because it does not link physical pliancy to mental pliancy in particular but only makes the general claim that virtuous physical activity is a support for virtuous mental activity.

I think, though, that a more substantive reading of Vasubandhu's claim is possible. If one's body is able to more easily engage in virtuous activity—such as caring for others—then there will be less psychological resistance to doing those activities. When one's body is not able to engage in caretaking activities without considerable pain and fatigue, it becomes more difficult to perform those activities, since the negative physical experience makes it that much more likely that we will develop psychological aversion to the virtuous activity. Insofar as mental pliancy is about overcoming psychological resistance (aversion or dislike) to directing one's mind toward virtue, then physical pliancy is a favorable condition that is directly supportive of mental pliancy *in particular*. Having physical pliancy prevents a major source of psychological resistance, the aversion to pain, fatigue, and other physical discomfort involved in caring for others.

66 THE VIRTUE OF OPEN-MINDEDNESS

Vasubandhu's discussion of physical pliancy raises a broader philosophical question for understanding open-mindedness: to what extent is OM conditioned by the practices, habits, limitations, and potentialities of the body? And, if Vasubandhu is correct that physical pliancy is a favorable condition for the cultivation of OM, what does that mean for the understanding how OM is cultivated? The inclusion of physical pliancy also raises a question—which is not discussed by Vasubandhu: how does mental pliancy or OM affect one's experience of one's body? These are not merely academic questions. Recent research by Owens et al. on chronic pain patients suggests those who were "adaptive" (rather than "distressed") tended to score high on the scale that measures "openness," a trait that includes the "willingness to try new behaviors and consider new ideas" (Owens et al. 2016, 27). Adaptiveness to physical pain, according to this study, is highly correlated to something like open-mindedness or mental pliancy, although the causal relation between these traits is unclear. It is not clear whether, as Vasubandhu's claim would suggest, the patients who were able to gain some degree of physical pliancy (the "adaptive" patients) thereby created a favorable condition for mental pliancy ("openness"), or whether the mentally pliancy of the patients is what allowed them to recognize or reconceive the serviceability (pliancy) of their bodies. At the very least, though, studies like this urge us to follow these Buddhist philosophers' lead in taking seriously the relationship between physical and mental pliancy, that is, to take seriously the embodied nature of OM.

1.3 The Affective Dimensions of Pliancy and Open-Mindedness

As we have already seen, the function of pliancy is to overcome negative tendencies that cause us to dislike bringing our attention to a particular object. These negative tendencies—conceived of in terms of aversion, craving, and delusion—are affective states that create affective barriers to the manifestation of mental pliancy. Mental pliancy is not only about the ability to take up novel, virtuous objects of thought but also about engaging the management and eventual elimination of the negative affective states that prevent such virtuous thought.

PERSPECTIVE-TAKING AND A FLEXIBLE MIND   67

There are at least two ways that pliancy functions in our affective lives. First, Buddhist moral psychology tends to highlight the ways that dysfunctional emotional habits, such as pride, greed, or envy, act as a kind of emotional stubbornness that can impede our ability to transcend our default cognitive standpoint. It is difficult to open-mindedly consider another cognitive standpoint when one has strong emotional resistance to that standpoint or strong emotional attachment to our default perspective. Consider "motivated cognition," the "inclination toward a set of beliefs if those beliefs seem to justify some other view that one wants to be true, or whose truth one is emotionally invested in" (Kelly, Foucher, and Machery, 298). White people in the United States, for example, often have a strong emotional investment in the belief that the United States is a meritocratic society. This strong emotional investment impedes their (our) ability to transcend that default cognitive standpoint and seriously consider the evidence that the United States is more accurately described as a white supremacist society (Mills 1997; Mills 2007; McRae 2016; McRae 2019).

The resistance to taking up a new cognitive perspective ("The United States is a white supremacy") that is different from one's default cognitive perspective ("The United States is a meritocracy") is mainly emotional. In such cases, too much is at stake, personally and emotionally, to divest, even temporarily, from our default standpoint. This emotional resistance is a serious threat to the cultivation of open-mindedness, as a moral or epistemic virtue, that needs to be accounted for in our conceptions of OM and in our understanding of how OM is developed or cultivated.[6]

For the Buddhist ethicists presented here, the default standpoints that we are transcending—and the new ones we are attempting to embody—are not only cognitive, but they are also (and sometimes, primarily) affective. This kind of affective open-mindedness is the second way that pliancy functions in our emotional lives. For example, resentment or envy can be a default standpoint that has cognitive and affective aspects; we see things from the point of view of one who is underappreciated or denied and experience the corresponding emotions. Pliancy is what allows for the relaxation of the rigidity of that affective standpoint, which is achieved by being open to other affective standpoints, usually compassion or love. Compassion and

68   THE VIRTUE OF OPEN-MINDEDNESS

love, on the Buddhist view, are not just feelings that we have—or even feelings coupled with characteristic thoughts and behaviors; they are orientations toward the world, affective and cognitive standpoints that motivate certain ways of thinking, speaking, and acting in the world. In order to take up such an affective standpoint and to integrate it into our habits of thinking, feeling, and action, we need a mind that is flexible and open.

2 Perspective-Taking and Transcending Default Standpoints

It is a reasonable assumption that one way to increase the mind's ability to take up new cognitive and affective standpoints (for the sake of developing oneself as a moral and epistemic agent) is to practice taking up perspectives that differ from or even oppose one's default perspective. Buddhist moral psychology is replete with practices designed to illustrate the moral and epistemic value of perspective-taking. There are, for example, perspective-taking exercises that encourage us to take the perspective of an animal led to slaughter, a criminal awaiting his sentence, a yak carrying a heavy load of tea across a steep mountain pass, and the labors of one's own mother (Patrul 1994, 195–217; Pelzang 2004, 136–151). Consider this perspective-taking exercise from the 19th-century Tibetan Buddhist thinker Patrul Rinpoche, which invites us to imagine ourselves as sheep awaiting slaughter.

> Think carefully about the suffering of these animals. Imagine that you yourself are undergoing that suffering and see what it is like. Cover your mouth with your hands and stop yourself breathing.[7] Stay like that for a while. Experience the pain and the panic. When you have really seen what it is like, think again and again how sad it is that all those beings are afflicted by such terrible sufferings without a moment's respite. (204)

This practice—and the many similar practices in Buddhist ethics—is not presented as a passing rhetorical device to provoke a burst of sympathy in the moment, but as a sustained ethical and epistemic practice

PERSPECTIVE-TAKING AND A FLEXIBLE MIND   69

designed to radically shift one's default cognitive and affective standpoint for the purpose of cultivating love, compassion, and wisdom. In the discussion of pliancy above, I located three important dimensions of pliancy: the moral dimension, the embodied dimension, and the affective dimension. This perspective-taking practice is an illustration of all three. The practice is clearly a moral practice, as its purpose is to motivate care and concern for other members of the moral community, which, for Patrul Rinpoche, includes animals. The affective dimensions of the practice are also significant. We are not primarily trying to cognitively understand what it might be like to be a sheep being slaughtered (it would, after all, be very hard to know that), but we are using this reflection in order to *feel* differently about harm done to members of the moral community. Through perspective-taking, we are first and foremost aiming to embody a new affective standpoint, one of compassionate concern. The practice also includes an embodied aspect of pliancy: by advising us to restrict our own breath to "experience the pain and the panic," Patrul Rinpoche is making use of the body as a support to changing one's default perspective.

According to Buddhist moral psychology, perspective-taking practices serve as antidotes to apathy and cruelty because they can undercut the cognitive/affective standpoints that give rise to these moral faults. The main cognitive/affective standpoint that causes apathy, cruelty, and other moral vices, for Buddhist ethicists, is the self-centered standpoint. Such a standpoint can manifest in different ways, which is one reason that it can be difficult to detect, especially in oneself. Patrul Rinpoche, following the great eighth-century Indian moral philosopher Śāntideva, understands the self-centered standpoint as fundamentally comparative; it gains momentum through comparison to others. This comparison can take three predictable forms: superiority, rivalry, and inferiority (Patrul, *Brightly Shining Sun*). The superiority oriented self-centered standpoint tends to see that others are worse than oneself, in some (or many!) domain(s), which produces a range of superiority-related faults, such as arrogance, vanity, and contempt. The rivalry-oriented form of self-centeredness sees others as competitors for resources and status, which leads to the faults of resentment, envy, and excessive competitiveness. The inferiority version of the self-centered standpoint sees others as inherently more

70 THE VIRTUE OF OPEN-MINDEDNESS

worthy, deserving, and successful than the self and leads to the typical inferiority faults of despondency, envy, lack of self-worth, and lack of motivation.

Unlike Western moral psychologies that tend to categorize inferiority vices as the natural opposites of superiority vices, Buddhist moral philosophers tend to see these faults as similar in kind. Just as false feelings of superiority are indicative of an unhealthy and morally problematic obsession with the self (an obsession with how great one takes oneself to be in comparison to others), false feelings of inferiority are also indicative of an unhealthy and morally problematic obsession with the self (an obsession with one's perceived failures and inferiority in comparison with others). Despondency, on this view, is a self-centered state, as one has become fixated on one's own limitations and failures. In both the inferiority and superiority cases, the problem is fundamentally due to a myopic and warped perception of self in relation to others. This is why some Buddhist moral philosophers have classified self-loathing as a kind of conceit (Heim 2009).

Many Buddhist thinkers present perspective-taking practices as useful tools to undermine this most basic form of cognitive and affective rigidity: the self-centered standpoint. One of the most interesting and complex perspective-taking exercises in Indo-Tibetan Buddhist philosophy is "exchanging self and other." The following verses are instructions for the practice of exchanging self and other from the classic text of Buddhist moral philosophy, the *Bodhicaryāvatāra* (*The Bodhisattva's Way of Life*), by Śāntideva.

> VIII. 140 Creating a sense of self in respect of inferiors and others, and a sense of other in oneself, imagine envy and pride with a mind free from false notions!

Śāntideva is asking us to consider ourselves from the point of view of others, particularly inferiors (those who have less than we have on some scale and so are disposed to envy us), equals (our peers, those of the same status who are disposed to feel rivalry with us), and superiors (those who have more than we have and so are disposed to view us with contempt). This is an uncomfortable exercise, since these groups of people are likely to have negative views of us. (It is also one of the

PERSPECTIVE-TAKING AND A FLEXIBLE MIND 71

few times I have ever seen a Buddhist author suggest cultivating envy and pride.) But, thankfully, Śāntideva gives us a script. When taking up the perspective of an inferior who envies us, we think to ourselves:

> VIII. 141 He is honored, not I. I do not receive such alms as he. He is praised. I am criticized. I suffer. He is happy.
>
> VIII. 142 I do chores while he remains at ease. He, it seems, is great in the world. I, it seems, am inferior, without virtues.
>
> VIII. 146 He has no compassion for people who stand in the jaws of an evil rebirth. Moreover, out of pride in his virtues he longs to have victory over the learned.

Note that the "he" in these verses refers to the self, and the "I" refers to the other (which is why these sorts of practices are called "exchanging self and other"). We are trying to transcend the most basic default standpoint, our own self-conception, at least in terms of how we view our virtues and vices, successes and failures, and our place in our social world. We do this by taking on another—in this case oppositional—cognitive and affective standpoint: the point of view of others who are well-positioned to dislike us.

After viewing ourselves from the point of view of those who envy us—which encourages us to see our virtues and successes as undeserved, our good fortune as wasted on us, and our social persona as cold and uncaring—we move on to see ourselves from the point of view of those who feel rivalry with us (equals) and those who feel contempt for us (superiors). Śāntideva imagines that the very same other (who, remember, is "I" in this scenario) has had a change of fortune and becomes the superior:

> VIII. 148 Suppose my virtues were to become apparent to everyone in the world, then no one would even hear of his virtues.
>
> VIII. 149 Were my faults to be concealed there would be worship for me not for him. Now I receive gifts of alms easily. I am honored while he is not.
>
> VIII. 150 Delighted we shall watch while at last he is crushed, the object of everyone's ridicule, criticized from all sides.

72   THE VIRTUE OF OPEN-MINDEDNESS

> VIII. 152 Indeed, it seems this wretch once even vied with me! Does he have this much learning, wisdom, beauty good breeding, or wealth?

Here we are again asked to upend the default cognitive and affective standpoint of self-centeredness, but this time focus on challenging the narrative of ourselves as competent, accomplished, and deserving of all our successes. When taking up the perspective of a superior, someone who, because of arrogance, expresses disregard and contempt toward us, we see ourselves as ridiculous, ignorable, wretched, and pathetic. By moving through these (aversive) perspectives of ourselves, we are gaining the mental flexibility that is particularly relevant to the cultivation of open-mindedness: the ability to take seriously standpoints that are not just different from but oppositional to our default standpoint. In doing so, we learn to transcend our default cognitive/affective standpoint, which in this case is a complex one: a collection of thoughts, assumptions, narratives, and beliefs about who we are in relation to others.

We should keep in mind that exchanging self and others is a *practice*; it is what primes us for being able to abandon false narratives about ourselves that prevent us from considering new standpoints *when we need to do so*. It is about cultivating a skill of openness, or a disposition to be open. This is clear from the fact that we are being asked to take seriously *conflicting* narratives about ourselves—we are both arrogant and uncaring *and* contemptible and useless. This exercise is not about coming to understand who you *really* are but is a practice of being open and flexible with regard to some of your most cherished self-narratives in order to challenge the default habit of self-centeredness. It also shows us how much of "who we are"—our personality, our moral virtues, even our physical qualities—is defined with respect to the perspective from which they are viewed.

Usually when we talk about OM, we tend to focus on the ability to be able to seriously consider that a particular belief, even a deeply held one, may be wrong (Adler 2004; Riggs 2010). When confronted with evidence, the open-minded person could reconsider her assumptions about, say, what good parenting is or her belief that all members of the opposing political party are morally corrupt. But what Śāntideva

PERSPECTIVE-TAKING AND A FLEXIBLE MIND   73

is asking us to do is to be open-minded in a much more expansive, and more personal, sense. Exchanging self and other challenges our assumptions about who we are, how important or deserving we are, how we compare to others in our social world. The reason, I suspect, for this expansive and even radical OM is that Śāntideva is working with a more obviously moral framework than an epistemic one (although epistemic concerns are certainly not irrelevant). For Śāntideva, being able to consider new standpoints isn't only about getting closer to the truth, but it is also about being able to effectively care for others. And the close-minded, rigid, or lazy assumptions that keep us from caring for each other usually have to do with deeply ingrained, emotionally laden views about our own worth and place in our social world. Or, at least, that seems to be Śāntideva's working hypothesis.

3 Objections

I conclude by briefly responding to some recent objections to perspective-taking as a moral practice. First, we may worry that taking up another's perspectives may not be possible or, even when it is possible, it may not be morally desirable. In her critique of perspective-taking as an impartiality practice, Marilyn Friedman discusses the case of taking up the evil or perverse perspectives, such as trying to see the world the way a child molester might see it. It is doubtful that we could understand the motives, desires, and actions of a child molester as he himself sees them (at least, in relation to the molestation of children; we may more easily relate to other aspects of his psychology). But, and this is Friedman's main point, even if we could take up such a perspective, it is unclear why, morally speaking, we would want to (Friedman 1993, chapter 2).

There is a basic worry here about the ways that perspective-taking can obscure rather than clarify moral obligations. By taking up the wrong perspectives, we may come to empathize with wrongdoing in a way that obscures its wrongness and lessens our resolve to take proper action. Because we do not want to minimize the wrongness of child molestation for the child, who is the most vulnerable party, we do not want to take up the perspective of the wrongdoer. The empathy we

74   THE VIRTUE OF OPEN-MINDEDNESS

have for the wrongdoer may have the effect of limiting the empathy we have for the victim, and, sensibly, we don't want to take that risk. This danger of empathic perspective-taking has been recently exposed by public conservations surrounding the #metoo movement. As I see it, one of the aims (and successes) of the movement was to expose how much more quickly and robustly our society tends to empathize with the perspectives of those *accused* of sexual harassment than with the perspectives of the victims of it, a phenomenon Kate Manne has coined "himpathy" (Manne 2017). Taking seriously this morally problematic tendency, we might do well to limit our perspective-taking with the accused in order take seriously the claims of the victims.

I generally agree with this kind of worry about perspective-taking as an ethical practice, especially as an impartiality practice (McRae 2013). But I don't think that Buddhist accounts such as Śāntideva's are particularly susceptible to them. First, as I mentioned earlier, Buddhist perspective-taking practices are embedded in a fairly explicit moral framework and have clear moral aims, such as to develop compassion and wisdom, and to overcome self-absorption. The ability to identify with any perspective whatsoever is not valued (at least, I've never seen a Buddhist philosopher praise this general skill), but rather we *select* perspectives to consider based on moral values and our moral self-knowledge. In fact, Buddhist philosophers often select for us perspectives that will likely encourage the development of compassion and self-knowledge—for example, Patrul Rinpoche's suggestion to take up the perspective of an animal about to be slaughtered. These kinds of exercises are designed to expose and correct for a typical human moral failure, in this case the disregard of animal suffering. A perspective-taking exercise that simply reinforced morally problematic bias or distracted us from urgent moral obligations would not serve its purpose and so would not be encouraged in Buddhist ethics.

It is important to note that Buddhist perspective-taking practices are highly contextualized. It is because we usually ignore, wrongly, the suffering of animals that we should direct our minds toward it. Similarly, since we usually underestimate, wrongly, the harms of being sexual harassed, we should direct our minds toward those harms. The perspective-taking practices are functioning as correctives to our biases or, at least, giving us knowledge that such biases are present in

PERSPECTIVE-TAKING AND A FLEXIBLE MIND   75

us. In the case of the child molester, because of the severity of the harm, the long-term impact of the wrongdoing, and the high degree of vulnerability of the victim, our first moral obligation is clearly to the child who is the victim. For that reason, we should direct our minds to the harms suffered by the victim. But, in certain contexts, Buddhist ethical views would also support taking up the perspective of the child molester—for instance, when developing therapeutic interventions for pedophilia. In such contexts it might be helpful to consider some relevant aspects of the child molester's experience of himself, such as what triggers or enables his pedophilia, in order to prevent future wrongdoing. The normative limit of pliancy or open-mindedness becomes important here; attempting to take up the perspective of a child molester is encouraged only insofar as doing so would prevent further wrongdoing.

The second main worry about the ethics of perspective-taking is more foundational. Whether it is morally beneficial to take up the perspectives of others may be a moot point, since our assumption that we can accurately understand others through perspective-taking is unfounded. Psychological research suggests that we are poor at projecting ourselves into the situations of others because we imagine these situations in a crude, "card-board cut-out" way, in a way that is "naked, decontextualized [and] prototypical" (Maibom 2013, 513). The problem isn't just about understanding the perspectives of others; we often fail to accurately predict how we ourselves would react in a hypothetical situation (Maibom 2013, 511). For these reasons, Heidi Maibom has argued that prioritizing perspective-taking as a primary ethical practice is misguided.

I agree with Maibom that, if our goal is to understand and gain knowledge about what another person would do in a given situation—to predict their actions—then perspective-taking may not be as helpful as we might assume, for the reasons that she gives. But I doubt that gaining knowledge about other's motivations or actions is the goal of the perspective-taking practices in South Asian Buddhist ethical traditions. Rather, it seems to me that the aim of these practices is the transformation of the self through revealing one's biases and aversions and making oneself better acquainted with one's own moral tendencies. In Śāntideva's case, the goal of exchanging self and other

76 THE VIRTUE OF OPEN-MINDEDNESS

is not to accurately understand or predict the motivations of another person, since we are imagining a person who does not exist. In this exercise, we do not bring to mind an actual person who envies us and try to accurately predict his motivations or decision-making procedures. We are not making predictions through perspective-taking but rather doing a kind of self-inquiry through the mechanism of imaginatively seeing ourselves through the perspective of a fictional other. The goal is moral self-transformation.

To summarize, I've argued for the following three claims. First, Buddhist accounts of pliancy overlap with contemporary Western accounts of open-mindedness in that they have similar functions—the consideration of new perspectives, the flexibility of thinking—and are opposed to similar vices—rigidity, dogmatism, narrow-mindedness, laziness. Second, Buddhist accounts of pliancy and Western OM are nevertheless differently oriented, and understanding them in dialogue can reveal possible aspects of OM that would otherwise be obscured. These include the moral dimensions of OM, the importance of the pliancy of the body for understanding the pliancy of the mind, and relevance of an affective OM. Third, mental pliancy or OM (both cognitive and affective) can be cultivated through perspective-taking practices, which (i) seek to challenge our self-centered standpoints, and so are (ii) explicitly normative and (iii) function for the purpose of self-inquiry rather than the accurate prediction of others' behaviors.

Notes

1. There are some exceptions: Arpaly 2011, McRae 2016, and Cremaldi and Kwong 2017 focus on OM as a moral virtue.
2. For discussion on OM's conductivity to truth, see Kwong 2017.
3. The Abhidharma is an early collection of texts that attempt to systemize the teachings of the Buddha, and is focused on constructing a Buddhist philosophy of mind and psychology, as well as a Buddhist ontology. Here I focus on the Sarvāstivādin Abhidharma tradition, although there is a similar concept—malleability (*mudutā*)—in the Pali Abhidhamma tradition (see Buddhaghosa PP XIV.146).
4. The other ten are (1) faith, (2) dignity, (3) propriety, (4) non-attachment, (5) non-aggression, (6) non-confusion, (7) diligence, (8) conscientiousness, (9) equanimity, (10) non-harmfulness.
5. Thanks to Seth Robertson for bringing up this example.
6. In a previous article, I argued that Buddhist conceptions of equanimity—freedom from craving and aversion—are helpful for understanding OM (McRae 2016). When we are simply reacting to our cravings and aversions there is little cognitive or affective space to try out a new perspective.

PERSPECTIVE-TAKING AND A FLEXIBLE MIND   77

7. The reason the Patrul Rinpoche suggests restricting one's own breath is because in Tibet animals were slaughtered by suffocating them.

Works Cited

Adler, Jonathan. 2004 "Reconciling Open-Mindedness and Belief." *Theory and Research in Education* 2(2) (July): 127–142. https://doi.org/10.1177/147787850 4043440.

Arpaly, Nomy. 2011. "Open-mindedness as a Moral Virtue." *American Philosophical Quarterly* 48 (January): 75–85.

Asanga. 2015. *Abhidharmasamuccaya: The Compendium of Higher Teaching*, trans. Sara Boin-Webb and Walpola Rahula. Fremont, CA: Jain Publishing.

Baehr, Jason. 2011. "The Structure of Open-Mindedness." *Canadian Journal of Philosophy* 41(2): 191–213. https://doi.org/10.1353/cjp.2011.0010.

Cremaldi, Anna and Jack M. C. Kwong. 2017. "Is Open-Mindedness a Moral Virtue?" *Ratio* 30(3): 343–358. https://doi.org/10.1111/rati.12149.

Friedman, Marilyn. 1993. *What Are Friends For?* Ithaca: Cornell University Press.

Hare, William. 2006. "Why Open-Mindedness Matters." *Think* 5(13): 7–16. https://doi.org/10.1017/S1477175600001482.

Heim, Maria. 2009. "The Conceit of Self-Loathing." *Journal of Indian Philosophy* 37(1): 61–74.

Kelly, Daniel, Luc Faucher, and Edouard Machery. 2010. "Getting Rid of Racism: Assessing Three Proposals in Light of Psychological Evidence: Getting Rid of Racism." *Journal of Social Philosophy* 41(3): 293–322. https://doi.org/ 10.1111/j.1467-9833.2010.01495.x.

Kwong, Jack M. C. 2016. "Open-Mindedness as a Critical Virtue." *Topoi* 35(2): 403–411. https://doi.org/10.1007/s11245-015-9317-4.

Kwong, Jack M. C. 2017. "Is Open-Mindedness Conducive to Truth?" *Synthese* 194(5): 1613–1626. https://doi.org/10.1007/s11229-015-1008-6.

Lodrö, Geshe Gendun. 1998. *Calm Abiding and Special Insight: Spiritual Transformation through Meditation.* Ithaca: Snow Lion.

Maibom, Heidi L. 2013. "Limits of Perspective Taking." *Procedia—Social and Behavioral Sciences*, The 9th International Conference on Cognitive Science, 97 (November): 511–516. https://doi.org/10.1016/j.sbspro.2013.10.266.

Manne, Kate. 2017. *Down Girl: The Logic of Misogyny.* New York: Oxford University Press.

McRae, Emily. 2013. "Equanimity and Intimacy: A Buddhist-Feminist Approach to the Elimination of Bias." *Sophia* 52(3): 447–462. https://doi.org/10.1007/s11 841-013-0376-y.

McRae, Emily. 2016. "Equanimity and the Moral Virtue of Open-Mindedness." *American Philosophical Quarterly* 53(1): 97–108.

McRae, Emily. 2019. "White Delusion and Avidyā: A Buddhist Approach to Understanding and Deconstructing White Ignorance." In *Buddhism and Whiteness: Critical Reflections*, ed. Emily McRae and George Yancy. Lanham, MD: Lexington Press.

Mills, Charles. 1997. *The Racial Contract.* Ithaca: Cornell University Press.

78 THE VIRTUE OF OPEN-MINDEDNESS

Mills, Charles. 2007. "White Ignorance." In *Race and Epistemologies of Ignorance*, ed. Nancy Tuana and Shannon Sullivan (pp. 11–38). Albany: State University of New York Press.

Owens, Justine E., Martha Menard, Margaret Plews-Ogan, Lawrence G. Calhoun, and Monika Ardelt. 2016. "Stories of Growth and Wisdom: A Mixed-Methods Study of People Living Well with Pain." *Global Advances in Health and Medicine* 5(1): 16–28. https://doi.org/10.7453/gahmj.2015.065.

Pelzang, Khenpo Ngawang. 2004. *A Guide to The Words of My Perfect Teacher*. Boston: Shambala.

Powers, John. 1995. *Introduction to Tibetan Buddhism*. Ithaca: Snow Lion.

Riggs, Wayne. 2010. "Open-Mindedness." *Metaphilosophy* 41(1–2): 172–188. https://doi.org/10.1111/j.1467-9973.2009.01625.x.

Rinpochay, Lati Rinpochay and Denma Lochö. 1997. *Meditative States in Tibetan Buddhism*. Boston: Wisdom Publications.

Rinpoche, Mipham. 1997. *Gateway to Knowledge*, vol. 1. Hong Kong: Rangjung Yeshe Publications.

Rinpoche, Patrul. n.d. "Brightly Shining Sun." *Lotsawa House*. http://www.lotsawahouse.org/bo/tibetan-masters/patrul-rinpoche/bodhicharyavatara-brightly-shining-sun. Accessed September 14, 2018.

Rinpoche, Patrul. 1994. *The Words of My Perfect Teacher*. Lanham, MD: Altamira Press.

Śāntideva. 1995. *The Bodhicaryāvatāra*, trans. Kate Crosby and Andrew Skilton. New York: Oxford University Press.

Vasubandhu. 2012. *Abhidharmakośa-bhāṣya*, ed. Gelong Lodrö Sangpo (trans.), vol. 1. Delhi: Motilal Banarsidass Publishers.

Zahler, Leah. 2009. *Study and Practice of Meditation: Tibetan Interpretations of the Concentrations and Formless Absorptions*. Ithaca: Snow Lion.

3

A Trickster's Sideways Look at Open-Mindedness as a Virtue: A Native American Perspective

Rockey Robbins and Howard Bad Hand

1 A True Native American Story

After we accepted the invitation to write about the concept of open-mindedness as a virtue, I (one of the authors of this chapter) had supper with three Native American friends. When one asked what we were writing about and I responded, "open-mindedness," I was met with a cavalcade of humorously sarcastic remarks. "Sounds like white people wanting to scalp Indians again to me. Did they offer you insurance for opening up your head on that topic?" Another said, "Yea, wonder how many times in history white people have asked Indians to be open-minded about church and government and land and culture." "Did they tell you what kind of open-mindedness they wanted from you because they already cut my mind open and stuffed so much in there that I can't tell what is Indian and what is white anymore?" "I agree, in fact, they done opened up 'bout everything there is in me from my head to my ass and took out everything and replaced it with their open-mindedness." The conversation became progressively more funny and filthy, and sadly I can't remember many of the hilariously brilliant remarks they made.

2 Introduction: The Writing Approach

Let us begin with a critical consciousness about the concept of open-mindedness, being careful to correct cognitive distortions and

Rockey Robbins and Howard Bad Hand, *A Trickster's Sideways Look at Open-Mindedness as a Virtue: A Native American Perspective* In: *The Virtue of Open-Mindedness and Perspective.* Edited by: Wayne D. Riggs, Oxford University Press. © Oxford University Press 2025. DOI: 10.1093/9780190080723.003.0004

80   THE VIRTUE OF OPEN-MINDEDNESS

recognizing the contexts of colonization. An honest reflection upon the idea of open-mindedness requires that we engage in a decolonization project that will involve challenging neo-liberal models of argumentation else it will be conscripted into a settler-colonial pattern of thinking. We, as Native Americans, are constantly being positioned to comprehend existence through the eyes of anti-indigeneity, which entails the enactment of epistemic violence through mis-naming, erasure, and discounting of our ways of being Native Americans (Smith 2013). Grosfoguel (2007) argues that failing to resist hegemonic, asymmetrical global power relations embedded in argument organization sustains a dominant North American–centric epistemology claiming to be authoritative, universal, and science-based, contributing to the erosion of the confidence of colonized groups in their self-efficacy and academic performances. In this chapter, we attempt to situate the ways in which the values of rationalism, objectivity, and agonism contribute to ongoing Native American genocide and discuss how "virtues," in particular open-mindedness, get situated within the libidinal economy of violence, describing how certain groups have the power to over-determine how virtue is defined, what it is, and who can be described as virtuous. Consequently, we will take into account communicative, historical, and social processes, and we will utilize Native American communicative approaches to combat the accretions of malevolence embedded in raced language, thought, and writing patterns.

First, it must be acknowledged that for us (the Native American writers of this text) to relate to our audience at all, we must interact verbally and in written form and in a language foreign to us. Our cultural capital, our languages, rhetorical style, epistemologies, and our land, are not and cannot be recognized if the continuity of the colonizing system is to be sustained (Wolfe 2006). George J. Sefa Dei explains, "Indigenous ways of knowing are based on 'an understanding of the spiritual sense of the self and the collective'" (Dei 2006, 5). He argues that settler ways of knowing dislocate Native American peoples' lifeways and storytelling traditions. He writes that settler rhetorical strategies must be resisted with discursive traditions that draw upon "multiple knowing, subjectivity, positionality, location, and history" (Dei 2006, 3). To achieve a Native American perspective necessarily entails challenging not only the objective, logical content of Western ideologies, the epistemologies and hegemonies of Western colonialism but also the modes of expressing ideas that are also assumed by colonizers as psychologically and ideologically superior. It also involves our (writers of this chapter) own liberation from the colonizers' view of our being childlike/childish/uncivilized in our means and mode of expression (Moane 1999; Nandy 2009).

Knowing that our tribal ways of organizing and reflecting upon ideas are construed differently from most Euro-American conceptions, as we begin writing, we wonder whether the editors will confer a settler order upon our ideas in their efforts to make our ideas intelligible for the general reader. How open-minded will they be to our ways of construing the world? For instance, the quandary we find ourselves in is that we are not in a position to engage an audience in an oral fashion (nor in our own tribal languages). All of the authors are highly aware of the lack of presence that characterizes written communication. Readers do not hear the tone, tempo, and volume of our voices nor see the gestures and facial expressions in our enactments; nor do we experience the readers' presences. Analysis of the written words in this chapter is detached from the embodiment of our physical presence. We have dared to write this chapter in a way, much of it in dialogue form, that attempts to honor our oral ways of communication. The dialogue form we present respects the polyvocal relational way of what we value in our communications. We offer songs and stories in written form as means of argumentation.

We also explore various dimensions of the concept of open-mindedness by discussing its utility in exploring our people's efforts to ensure that our ceremonies meet our current needs, in promoting healthy relationships and the expansion of our awareness, and in considering how, when assumed as a life principle, it is potentially detrimental to living life authentically and spontaneously.

3 Trickster Analytic Approach

We utilize a trickster analytic as one of our approaches for developing our ideas rather than a linear form of rational argumentation. This does not mean that what we are saying is irrational or nonsense. It

82 THE VIRTUE OF OPEN-MINDEDNESS

is simply a tribal way of making our points. If you were to ask Native Americans what characteristic defines them more than anything else, most would say their unique Native American sense of humor. Vine Deloria, Jr. wrote, "It has always been a great disappointment to Indian people that the humorous side of Indian life has not been emphasized by professed experts . . . Indians have found a humorous side to nearly every problem. . . . The more desperate the problem the more humor is directed to describe it " (Deloria 1988). Gerald Vizenor (Vizenor 1993) has been the most adept Native American to use humor to open our own and colonists' minds about our Native American predicament, including the milieu of White virtues and concepts imposed upon us. He follows the code of the Native American trickster to implode the status quo with blasphemous words that help us to consider the validity of ideas we have come to believe are conclusive. In his short film (1984), *Harold of Orange* he says, "The trickster was driven out of the land by the white man, who claimed the earth as his own. . . Tricksters are determined to reclaim their estate from the white man, challenging his very foundations." He argues that white people are not really interested in Native Americans unless they conform to general "white" fantasies. He says that white people get angry at and reject Native Americans who express their own truths and typically will search out Native Americans who are more likely to suit their purposes. All Native Americans must engage in trickster roles (even those in academia) because we are not in charge of our own existences. For instance, editors privilege writing for mainstream audiences. Consequently, Native American writers must humorously "sidestep" all questions put to them in such a way as to preserve some sort of dignity by addressing the racial and tribal issues that all questions are ultimately situated in. By humorous sidestepping, Native Americans can position themselves and demonstrate ironic elements in any White concept once it is placed in the context of a people whose cultural capital has been stolen.

When I first asked Howard Bad Hand, the revered Lakota Sundance Chief and singer, about what he thought about "being open-minded," he began to laugh and sidestepped the question a little, I assumed to gain the needed space to address the topic in a genuine way. I asked what was funny and he said, **"Laughing is being open-minded."** Then he said, **"I don't think of myself as being open-minded. I don't live**

A TRICKSTER'S SIDEWAYS LOOK   83

my life according to a tag. I laugh a lot because I am open to the moment I am living. As soon as you think of yourself as being open-minded you are already closing yourself off from it by trying to live inside a concept, a principle. . . . Now if you are laughing at something, aggressively putting it down, that is not open-mindedness either. But living life with a sense of humor . . . that is, allowing yourself to be vulnerable and open rather than closed to this life, I think that is being open-minded. Life deserves a good laugh (laughs). Singing, laughing, and dancing is about re-birth, opening your eyes and seeing everything new. And when you laugh you are in the moment. You are living, not stewing over it, not stuck in your head. You are absorbed in the moment, kind of astonished. In that moment you get to be what you really always have been, a person open to life. Laughter uncovers the eternal quality of life."

If there is one way to describe the collective spirit of Native Americans, it is that we love to laugh, whether we are exchanging witty one-liners or telling a funny story in the driest way imaginable. Tribal elders from my tribes, Tsalagi and Chata, have told me that if we didn't have a sense of humor when we have suffered such terrible things, none of us would be left. In the face of persecution, exploitation, and genocide, a sense of humor has created a needed perspective on and an escape from our problems. Humor opens us up to seeing another side of things. Humor helps us to re-adjust and be open to the happenings of the moment. Bad Hand teaches us open-mindedness as it relates to the peeling away of the protective shell of self-consciousness. In the passage quoted above, Bad Hand adds the sacred pulsation of laughter to the descriptors of a life open to experience. Laughter disentangles the closed-in self-conscious ego and allows us to become innocent again in our delight.

I asked, "Could you elaborate on this humor as an element in open-mindedness as it relates to the traditions of Lakota Heyokas?" He said, **"I am not a Heyoka, but I am a Comic.** Then he guffawed. I asked, **"What do you mean?"** He said, **"They exist to show the contradictions of life, and they entertain. If you are going about trying to look at things as good, they show that you are actually looking at evil things. Heyokas show the intermix of good and evil in all things, and they use humor to open your mind. Some of the young**

84   THE VIRTUE OF OPEN-MINDEDNESS

ones today are too aggressive and straightforward. Laughter is being vulnerable and open to the multiplicity of life, unlike worry and depression that is part of being self-enclosed. But Heyokas help us by not trying to do what we might think they should do. Again, being truly open minded is to live spontaneously, not according to principles or concepts, or in an overly calculated way. Heyokas are not functionally trying to open our minds. They are being humorous. They are being a balance for all of us and themselves in their contrariness. Humor is one of the great foods of life. It nourishes our souls. Laughter helps us to be more open minded about the changes that are always occurring around us, even the tragic ones. It helps us to adapt to the worst things that confront us. It does not mean that we are escapist and do not challenge wrongs. But with humor you can maintain a greater sense of harmony and it will help you from being so close-minded, controlling and rigid. Our ways of being funny keep us connected to our natural selves as Native Americans."

Bad Hand claims that humor can help us to see the oneness of apparent opposites, such as good and evil. Anxiety and sadness can interfere with being open to seeing the nuanced and seemingly contradictory meanings of our experiences. Gerald Vizenor explains that tricksters are voices that emerge from oral comic traditions that speak always in social situations and in dialogue, never in isolation or monologue and whose performance outcome opens new perspectives about the world (Vizenor 1993, 193). The trickster resists all attempts at monologue, comically reveals power relations, finds "loose seams and wild places" to plant seeds to open audience members' minds (Vizenor 1993, 196). The wisdom tricksters express comes out of lived experience, "never from following a lesson plan" (Vizenor 1993, 200). Their performance is an event, never isolated and self-contained like printed words. It is a dialogic experience (Vizenor 1993, 201). For the trickster, laughter, humor, and irony permeate every living interaction. To put things in print is to detach the hearer from the knower.

Some of the most poignantly comic performances Native American tricksters engage in is satirizing the social category and symbol of "whiteness." It is a playful way of opening our minds up and freeing them from what many white people expect us to conform to. Keith Basso's classic anthropological study, *The Portraits of the Whiteman*, reported that Native Americans regularly engage in interactions with the express purpose of encouraging their tribal people not to behave like "white people." Possibly the most common kind of joking the Native Americans does is exaggerated imitations of "white people's" "rigidity, greediness, intellectual superiority, advice giving, bossiness, harshness, over-gushy expressions of appreciation, and hasty friendships." The trickster knows that his or her representations are hyperbole and caricature, else they would be taken for their face value and would no longer be funny and might be met with resistance. These jokes are performed typically among Native American people and are viewed as ways of opening the assimilated Native Americans' eyes to seeing their real Native American selves are different from "white people."

I asked Bad Hand about Native Americans engaging in a conversation with white folks about open-mindedness. He said, **"White people are not open-minded. . . . That is a serious joke. . . .** (He then laughed hysterically, while I stuttered and offered a muted laugh.) He continued, **I look at what it isn't first. You cannot enact open-mindedness when you are pitted against aggressive closed-mindedness. We've not been put in a position to be open-minded. We were forced into accepting certain conditions without even being able to say 'no.' As persons who assume their ways are correct, white people are not in a position to be open-minded either. One must be in a position to want to learn in order to be open-minded. We have been in the position of being coerced with the consequence of misfortune if we do not do things as they want us to do. The thing of force has been on the side of white people. A person must be genuinely curious to have an open mind."**

Often, we as Native Americans are asked about our views about a given topic, with the assumption being that we are in a non-genocidal time for our tribal people. Most people acknowledge that Euro-Americans oppressed Native Americans in the past. They distinguished between themselves (human beings) and Native Americans (others and savages), paving the way to taking away land, declaring that Native Americans' labor was not work, declaring Native Americans incompetent, and justifying the imposition of their belief systems and extermination (Smith 2013). Genocide is waged against

86   THE VIRTUE OF OPEN-MINDEDNESS

Native Americans today in the form of low life expectancy, police brutality, overt and covert prejudice, lack of respect of our spiritual and intellectual perspectives and onto-epistemological conflicts. For Native Americans to write about anything, including open-mindedness, is to begin with the awareness that we write in the context of a world of ideas constructed in a settler colonial state, which de-values Native American knowledge (Dancy 2018).

It is necessary to think of open-mindedness as something that contains within itself a denotative insecurity, else exchange of ideas is not possible. Wayne Riggs argues that open-mindedness requires us to be "prepared to take seriously the views of others, especially when those views are in conflict with one's own"(Riggs 2010, 177). This viewpoint is in line with Jason Baehr's definition that an open-minded person "is characteristically (a) willing and (within limits) able (b) to transcend a default cognitive standpoint (c) in order to take up or take seriously the merits of (d) a distinct cognitive standpoint" (Baehr 2011, 266). William Hare's position that an open-minded person "is disposed to revise or reject the position he holds if sound objections are brought against it, or, in the situation in which the person presently has no opinion on some issue, he is disposed to make up his mind in the light of available evidence and argument as objectively and as impartially as possible" (Hare 1979, 9).

While these characteristics of open-mindedness are integral, the rationality and objectivity with which they are elaborated have heretofore been expressed within Euro-American argumentative structures. When these assumptions are put into a settler/colonial context, the context of the ongoing efforts of the genocide of Native Americans, they must be re-costumed. For instance, room must be made for the inter-subjectivity inherent in storytelling and spiritual wisdom imparted by elders who carry the old ways with them. It would also have to make room for the humor of the trickster that always reminds us that the reasoning and objectivity we think we achieve is both limited and potentially prejudiced.

It has become popular in Western societies, at least at a theoretical level, to embrace an ethos of open-mindedness. Bad Hand is concerned that Native Americans may not be in a position to engage in a polyvocal discussion with persons who cannot acknowledge their privileged positions. There is the danger of an "intensifying spiral" of open-mindedness moving to its inversion and becoming an avenue for violence against Native Americans. As suggested in the story that opened this essay, Native Americans clearly see serious implications about the relationship of open-mindedness to violence. Given that virtue ethics is profoundly focused on *arête*, *phronesis*, and *eudaimonia*, we are exploring how such a view of open-mindedness might necessarily be contradictory to these ideals in contexts involving Native Americans. We attempt to use Native American communication approaches and perspectives to rupture or at least expand open-mindedness as a virtue as it is typically conceived of by many Western ethicists.

4 Ceremony (Change and Conservation)

I told Bad Hand that I wanted to look at open-mindedness in a more concrete, practical way rather than just as a cerebral abstraction. Then I asked Bad Hand, **"What is the role that open-mindedness plays in regard to conducting ceremonies?"**

He said, **"We are taught to respect the old ways, but I am more interested in learning how to open up the way for Sun Dance to be conducted so that they speak to today's realities. I say, draw on the old but create new practices to meet the needs of the current time. I think it has always been this way. You'll find that if you talk to ten people who tell you that you must do the ceremony exactly this way or that, you will have been told ten different ways. I do what I think is the correct thing to do in the time I am in and sometimes other elders may not agree with me. I am open to the demand of the time in the time that it happens. . . . Open-mindedness requires that equally . . . to be open to the time, considering if it is right or wrong, whether it will help with learning, whether that which distinguishes it from the past would be dangerous to the participants. Proper limitations, repetitions can provide space for growth and expansion. But there is a balance, I will not conduct ceremonies that restrain thought and growth. We have a song that addresses this I believe. Think about the words of this old Lakota song."**

88 THE VIRTUE OF OPEN-MINDEDNESS

> **Kola, lecel ecun wo.** (Friend, do it this way.)
> **Lecanu ki,** (If you do it this way,)
> **Ni Tunkasila,** (Your Grandfather,)
> **Wani yank u kte lo.** (Will come to see you.)
> **Literalists take this song to mean to repeat endlessly the exact protocol of the ritual, but it is more than that. It is a metaphor for a way of being. Be in the here and now in the place of your voice, with the pipe, and you will connect with the past, present and future. The spirit world will unite with the material world if you are in a good way of being in a sweat lodge or at a Sun dance."**

Bad Hand is clear that he does not want to totally abandon the traditional form of the Sundance he leads. To lose too much of the form would be to lose the content of the Sun Dance as well. The form of Sun Dance defines to a large extent what the experience is for participants. But Bad Hand is also alert to whether the cultural/tribal ceremonies' forms are being enacted with relevant content. Even though changes might be needed, he moves cautiously because he knows that too drastic changes could be dangerous, as they could result in feelings of loss in terms of tribal identity. On the other hand, if the form of the ritual no longer speaks to the participants' needs yet it is repeated endlessly anyway, there is a danger of loss of participants' receptiveness to its supposed meaningfulness. Two years ago, a female cottonwood tree presented itself for sacrifice to a party of Sun Dancers. That same year, Bad Hand, resisting the traditionalists who argued that only males should carry the tree into the dance area, chose to have female dancers to carry the tree. His open-minded new enactment dissolved a long-standing custom at this Sun Dance. He was open to the rights of females: still, he conserved the way the tree was planted, dressed, and connected to the dancers.

In response to Bad Hand I remarked that I continue to encounter a great number of sweat ceremony participants arguing whether sweats today are either too stringent or too lax. Those who argue for stringency argue that the more lenient, the less likely healing spirits are to attend the meetings. Many are insistent that exact formalities should be adhered to. The less stringent argue that greater open-mindedness about how to conduct each sweat ceremony would contribute to meeting the unique needs of the participants.

While the new is necessary for creative and productive alterations to meet the needs of each generation, without some level of consistency in form, nothing substantial emerges. Form and dynamism are in continuous interaction. The form breaks the vital element of dynamic change, and the dynamism breaks the form. Without the form there is chaos and without the dynamism there is emptiness.

I asked, "How do I know that the changes are worth it?" Bad Hand said, **"It is a challenge to know. The old may have proven not to be useful so we open ourselves up to spirit who brings in new forms. Are we really striving humbly for the good? And are we holding back the new with old habits? A humble attitude is necessary, but it must be strong and adaptable if you really are committed to the new form. You must be selflessly resolute and consistent to work on it as long as it is useful. But the new is not always good. I question whether some of the new songs sung at Sun Dances are as helpful as the old ones that may be becoming forgotten."**

I responded, "But I thought open-ness to change in regard to ceremonies was vital to you, that worn-out traditions closed us off from being receptive to the needs of each new generation."

He said, **"There can be changes that are not useful and too much change directed by unwise persons can result in chaos. To be too much open-minded is equal to being closed-minded. If there were no boundaries and limits, everything would be drifting in an endless sea of unfulfilled possibilities, and there would be no relationships which limits provide for. Boundaries help us define. . . . There would be no distinctions in this reality that we occupy. We have to have order for any kind of movement forward. To be open-minded, you must strangely accept that this reality we live in is created by boundaries. Unlimited possibilities would make us dissolve into the boundlessness. It is all about balance."**

Like Bad Hand, my grandfather told me that it is vital to avoid extremes of reducing the ceremonies to an exactness. He told me that ceremonies should always be performed with a "freshness," but the basic elements of the ritual must not be discarded. For those who covet

90 THE VIRTUE OF OPEN-MINDEDNESS

exactness of the original ceremonial protocol actually mimicking "the first ritual" is dehumanizing because it takes away spontaneity and freedom to engage in imaginative creations. I understand that its general character can contribute to the security and harmony of a people who have been stripped of almost all of their cultural capital, but the character of sun dances and sweat ceremonies are composed of visionary elements that can never be utterly controlled by rigid rules. Open-mindedness is the portal for the freshness of transformation. To remain bound to the unchanging, we lose relevance and even pleasure. We cease to be a part of the unfolding creative wonder of living in this ever-changing world. The less stringent argue that the only way to survive is to re-imagine our sacred ways in our changing world.

On the other hand, too much of a commitment to change may hamper efforts to connect with something that is beyond any given temporal situation. Traditionalists may be right in emphasizing the unchangeable truth of the ceremonies they conduct. The traditionalist knows there are eternal messages within the forms through which they express their messages. Without this emphasis, the central tribal messages that are beyond any situation would be lost in the relativities of each new situation. There must be a measure of acceptance to the unchanging messages and the specific elements that make up the ceremonies.

I was curious as to what Bad Hand thought about the notion that some elders of different tribes believe in what one might call archetypal patterns established in pre-history and that these patterns should always be carried out to the letter. For them, ceremonies are events that help us to remember back to what has always been, before the beginning of time when human beings could experience an indescribable oneness. They believe some ceremonies can potentially help participants abolish profane time through their gestures, which help to transport participants into a relationship with a sacred event that was established before time began. I told Bad Hand that my grandfather taught me that in our sweat ceremonies participants are purified or regenerated by re-connecting with the unitary experience that supposedly existed before time. In a sweat ceremony, the leader will often begin the ceremony by explaining that the creation of the world is being reproduced. He taught me that the sweat ceremony re-enacts

A TRICKSTER'S SIDEWAYS LOOK   91

primordial events that took place before disharmony and imbalance emerged, reestablishing primordial unity and providing healing to all those who participate.

Bad Hand said, **"I have heard elders speak of what you are saying, and I would not argue with your grandfather. But I believe all of time is already here. Yes, remember all of this when you pray—the creation, the past, and Grandfather will come to see you. But spiritual reality is simultaneous with all of history, time. Spiritual wealth is all around us all the time, but we are not open to it. It seems funny to me to think of a time or no time before time.** (He began to laugh.) **It is easier for me to think of spiritual reality as being just always present, not before or after whatever."**

5 Open-Mindedness and Transpersonal Experience

I said, "This is connected to memory in some ways. So, let's talk about memory in its relationship to open-mindedness." He said, **"We create memory to try to hang on to experience. Then we try to explain the memory of a past experience and control its meaning. But it is important to keep the mind open to the present experience where there is stillness, instead of bringing stuff back. In Lakota, we say 'ekeek, suya.' It translates as 'memory,' or more literally, 'injury returns.' To be open to the totality of experience as it occurs, is to find balance and peace, even if it is for a short while. Reliving an experience over and over doesn't help you. Again, let me say reality is already here, always. When one finally 'gets there,' as they say, you are really here. You find it was always right here and right now, whether you are recalling an event or whatever."**

Memory keeps us closed off from the moment we are living in. It separates us from being where we are. To be in a state of memory we isolate or withdraw into a dark solitude and are unable to engage in the immediate surround. Only by being still within are we able to dissolve the barrier between the inside and outside. It is crucial for Bad Hand to be released from the tyranny of memory and its abstractions in order to open himself up to the ongoing process of life. For him, just as ceremonies that are endlessly repeated are parasitic ventures, so too is

92 THE VIRTUE OF OPEN-MINDEDNESS

drawing upon our past repeatedly because we close ourselves off from our wells of creativity. Instead of a dissolving flux in linear time which is grounded in memory, everything that has ever happened since the beginning of time is here and now.

I interpreted, "You seem to be getting into the area of transpersonal experience. Does your Native American spirituality include room for mind-expansion in terms of having visions, perceiving illnesses in others, communicating with spirits, experiencing an undivided connection with God? It is an area that many scientific minded people would not take seriously, yet it is something that many Native Americans see as important. How do you feel it is related to open-mindedness?"

He said, **"I believe rationalists and materialists who dismiss out of hand a spiritual, invisible reality are close-minded. To be truly open-minded one must acknowledge that there may be a reality our empirical perspective may not encompass. Some people put up the idea that this, what we see with our eyes, sense with our ears, nose, and touch, is the only reality. I see it as the only one many are willing to work with and show proof about, but there are those of us who know different realities, and we are not convinced that our tribal spiritual people are delusional. Prejudices, policing systems, are learned things. It becomes part of your experience and you feel you have control over it. If you are open-minded you can re-learn and create new experiences.**

The spirit world has a relationship with the material world. Open-mindedness loosens the door to spirit entities as well as our appearance in that world. To receive the voice of Tunkasila, I had to put away all rational thought, all analyzing and reasoning that I was using to try to understand. Those of us in touch with Spirit talk in terms of spirit energy and having conversations with sentient beings, sensing vibrations, interpreting energy. This connection to the Spirit World and spiritual beings can benefit this world. There is an ongoing interaction between this material world and the spiritual world. If you become selfless and less controlling, you become open to the Spirit's manifestation, and you become responsible for using the spiritual energy in a good way in this material world."

There is this opening up of awareness that is part of our Native American spirituality that is hard for many contemporary white people to comprehend as they see it as superstition. But it is a part of our traditional worldview which has been with us for centuries, and we are not about to let materialists take that cultural capital away from us. Bad Hand was especially emphatic about this. The Creator feeds us and we experience new awareness that we bring into our communities and it is given back to our Creator. As long as participants offer it back to the Creator, then there is a never-ending circular life to the energy. Only when one closes one's mind and becomes selfish is the life sustaining energy blocked. Blockage occurs when one becomes overly conscious, allowing a tyrannical controlling mind or selfish hoarding of the creative energy. In order to get the energy unblocked only requires going back to the original Energy Source through the original channels and spaces our ceremonies provide spaces for, but with what our elders advise repeatedly . . . with good thoughts, an open mind.

6 Relationships

I told Bad Hand that I had personally witnessed his leadership at Sundance, watching many people whom I would describe as individualists sharing in a good way and generously with each other during that week.

Bad Hand said, "**Lakota people are highly individualistic and competitive.**" I rejoined, "Native American peoples are usually categorized as collectivistic." He paused, then continued, "**Well, Lakotas are very competitive and often very separate from each other. I think that is why at Sun Dances they become so insistent on keeping every element of the ceremony the same year after year. They want to unite for that time with a single perspective on things. I think they have a deep belief, maybe unconscious, that keeping things the same will help with unity. There is a deep yearning to relate to each other and that has not been easy for us under the oppression we have endured because it separated us and made us compete for resources. But we share a reality together anyway. Ideally the dancers embrace every other dancer's prayers. This is how open-mindedness is created in**

94 THE VIRTUE OF OPEN-MINDEDNESS

the Sun Dance space. My goal is to be supportive, not telling anyone to dance this way or that. The point is not to change people but to share our lives with each other in a good way. Open-mindedness is a critical element of mitakuye oyasin, we are all related." I interjected, "Community is very important to you?" He said, "I like the word relationships better. I encourage the participants to help each other. Helping each other to cook, set up tents, carry the Sun Dance tree; all that helps to build relationships. People who come here to simply zone out and dance are acting individualistically. They would benefit from opening up their self-enclosed shells. You know, open up your mind and feed someone, buy someone lunch." He laughed, acknowledging that we had just bought him lunch.

Bad Hand leads by modeling and encouragement, careful not to violate each dancer's independence, but he tries to facilitate an independence from self-absorption. He sees the interdependence of individual freedom and the acknowledgment of everyone's needs for relationships. This interdependence exists on a mundane level, such as helping each other with camp chores, but also on a spiritual level in the form of embracing each other's prayers. The phrase, "We are all related" speaks in much more of an intimate way than the word collectivism or community. Bad Hand hopes that participants who help each other might transcend their enclosed existences to become open-minded. One of the Sun Dancers this year told me that he thought mitakuye oyasin was the single most important contribution that the Lakotas offered the world because it was an embodied teaching about opening our enclosed shells to connect with each other in both a spiritual and material way.

I asked Bad Hand about how dancing at a Sun Dance might facilitate open-mindedness. He said, "I have so far talked about how it is important to see open-mindedness in the context of being related to others, indeed all forms of life, and how learning to get along requires open-mindedness. In stillness, a person can feel their connection to others. In this openness we can 'make relations' or Wokakuye. The mind is joined with our social interaction. For harmony to emerge one must harmonize one's energies in a unity of effort. If you are in a combative or conflictual state you are not open to the transformational nature of reality. I tell the dancers to help each other, to fan off a person who appears to be getting too hot, to be where they are as they dance. Rather than spying into other people's business, [let them] dance their prayers."

The Sun Dance is about re-opening oneself up to authentic connections with others; it is about realizing oneself with the sense of belonging. It is about bonding with ancestors, co-participants and everything else. A basic Native American way of being is feeling and knowing we are indissolubly connected to others, to the earth, the cosmos and its circular rhythms. For those of us in academia, much of our energies subsume themselves in concepts, progress, development, and linear time. The Sun Dance is a way of experiencing life fully as it occurs. The sun dancers' enactment has always been and will always be in the moment. It is not abstract. It is dealing with experience in the sensuous/spiritual world that may lead us to re-inhabit time and space in a balanced way.

7 Open-Mindedness and Embodiment

I said, "I have always noted that when you talk about anything, you seem to quickly move away from purely abstract thinking. Is the concept of open-mindedness an abstract concept to you?" He said, "**Open-mindedness manifests itself when we realize the mind and body are one. I always tell my dancers that it is vital to dance their prayers. Dancing your prayers helps remove the conscious mind. Though it may be only for a brief moment, you find yourself not using your mind to interpret. You are in stillness and you are moving physically. In your still mind you are open to experiencing spiritual reality. In Lakota, the pipe is associated with Wowahwala, or stillness, which helps us to be in harmony with the emotional, mental, physical, and spiritual worlds. We don't fall into a trance to do this. We remain alert but our minds are still, that is not analyzing the experience, judging it. We harmonize our open-mindedness, receiving external stimuli, positively praying for others and combining that with the physical actions of dancing and singing.**"

To experience a Sun Dance ceremony in a holistic way is to keep the mind open to external stimuli, including the spirit world, and to put

96   THE VIRTUE OF OPEN-MINDEDNESS

forth goodness into the world. In the process, one may have a unitary experience, that is, feel a part of the immediate surround without the feelings of alienation that marks so much of our lives. Bad Hand does not dismiss the subjective aspect of open-mindedness as prayer. Bad Hand stresses that being open to the spirit world without concern or involvement in the external world may be an irrelevant subjective exercise. In this life that we live, there are ever-changing combinations of the elements of detached consideration and involvement. Balance is stressed. Bad Hand admonishes us to become more open to the awareness that inner and outer experiences are vital to our development. He does not advocate mindless trances; instead, you fill yourself with all the senses: sounds like the popping sounds of the rocks, the beating of the drums, the sweats scorching of the flesh, the taste of tobacco, the smells of cedar, and the taste of salt. You focus on what is happening. But eventually you are not an observer but part of the collective experience. In a sense, you merge with your surroundings, but you are mindful of it. The point is being in the place you are in in a good way. If you can find the place within you, you discover your nature without the mind claiming that it had done something. You don't hoard, hide or even defend your experience. You are not thinking in terms of progressing or developing or finding something eternal or permanent. You are alive with awareness, laughing often, constantly readjusting interrelationships with objects in your immediate surround. It is an openness to life.

I asked Bad Hand if he had anything else he would like to say about open-mindedness. He said, **"If there is anything Native Americans know from experience it is that the only constant is change. In fact, everything is changing all the time. Spirit says it didn't have beginning or end points, but somehow it got connected to matter to create the Universe that continues to keep expanding. Everything around me is changing. The property that White people own today may not continue to be theirs, and certainly not their distant forebears'. Cultural knowledge throughout history dissolves. In the meantime, some people can find peace, even those of us who resist the obliteration of our cultural knowledges. An open-minded person is curious about this changing existence. We have not always been open-minded to each other as tribes, but some great leaders were,**

A TRICKSTER'S SIDEWAYS LOOK 97

and some tribal groups have been. Sharing and opening up provides possibilities for growth, even harmony between groups. Curiosity involves an open-mindedness to learn something. But amidst this change, there is the possibility of being at peace with ourselves and to some extent with other people. Sun Dance helped me." (Bad Hand breathed deeply after this last statement.) Then he added, "I cannot tell anyone else how to do it, but maybe I can model what this means. . . . My Spirit guide, E. T., not Extraterrestrial (he smiles) but Eagle Thunder, has me conducting 16 years of Sun Dances at Sun Eagle Grounds to help people get to this peace. But then after sixteen years, I will let it go. Many people hold on to things beyond their usefulness, and consequently, they lack a peaceful and open mind. Open-mindedness is ultimately about having peace of mind in spite of being buffeted by negative experiences."

In the above remark, Bad Hand wrestles with balancing "the Lakota way" with meeting the current needs of the dancers at the Sun Dance he leads. He has always seemed to be mindful of vanishing points and vicissitudes. Continuity in his dances is guided by the Lakota religion, but he does not view the demise of specific "rules" as tragic. He often says that the main purpose of the Sun Dance he leads is peace. He once danced in the historical lands of the Lakota in South Dakota, but he re-located it to Arizona. "Rules," such as dancers must dance four-year stints or that only men can carry the sun dance tree into the dance area, he simply dismisses because history has altered the needs of people. He has written a song that includes both Navajo stanzas and Lakota stanzas, though some refuse to sing it. He says that needs of people and the world change, and he prizes good relationships between tribes. The Sun Dance remains significant for providing a space for peace and as long as it does it should be utilized, but he says he is always open-minded to changes that may facilitate inner and outward peace. He emphasizes how many of us experience a lack of peace, possibly we despair because of our lack of openness to the transitoriness of life. Though we try to prolong desirable stretches of time, it is to no avail. Imperialistic endeavors to secure spaces, an everlasting home, are inevitably defeated, whether one is Native American or white. For Bad Hand, peace can be found within, even for Native Americans who are largely in a current state of up-rootedness. For Bad Hand,

98 THE VIRTUE OF OPEN-MINDEDNESS

open-mindedness is the flexible, adaptable, and renewing aspect of healing.

8 Conclusion

This chapter began with the argument that the concept of open-mindedness originated and continues to be espoused in untenable contexts for Native Americans. Next, following the lead of other Native American theorists, we attempted to argue for a Native American rhetorical practice that might be more appropriate for Native Americans. For example, Christie Toth wrote, "All rhetorical situations in the United States are, by dint of their location, part of the settler colonial situation" (Toth 2016, 497) and argues that Native American rhetorical practices provide interpretive frames that persuade. Rachael Jackson added that allowing for "Native American cultural and rhetorical practices opens space for collaborative work... disrupting hegemonic abstraction" (Jackson 2017, 499). By employing the trickster dialectics of Gerald Vizenor (Vizenor 1993), that is, the use of irony, alternative perspectives in tension with normative ones hopefully allowed for a more flexible and pragmatic Native American understanding of the concept of open-mindedness. Bad Hand and I also considered open-mindedness in the light of the idea of being with others, mitokye oyasin. That is, the basic understanding of human beings as being immersed in constitutive relationships out of which an open mind is likely to recognize responsibility for others. This awareness is weighed against and overrides the notion of individualism. Creating webs of relationships and feeling empathy and curiosity about others' well-being or, acknowledging kinship, opens us up to individual transformation and also leads to new and creative social interactions and systems. Further, the spiritual dimension or an intuitive openness to heightened awareness addressed in this chapter may lead to an attunement to the unity of all reality. Open-mindedness was associated with expansion and enlargement, new beginnings and creativity, both in individual affirmations and ceremonial gatherings. There are cycles of opening and closing, expanding and contracting. A balance is needed. A person or a group may open at a rate that their system cannot accommodate or conversely contract to the extent that they cut themselves off from growth. Change is needed for growth, but it must be psychologically manageable and the core must be protected against incoherence.

It is hoped that the explorations into open-mindedness in this chapter have pointed in some new directions for persons experimenting with the expanding and contracting ideas related to open-mindedness. There was an attempt to elucidate readers about both the oppressive contexts as well as the problematic modes of expression Native Americans encounter when writing about virtues in general. The dialogic mode of discourse and the pragmatic focus on open-mindedness as it manifests in Native American life hopefully both honored Indigenous ontologies and shed light on nuances that may be overlooked in many considerations of the concept of open-mindedness.

Works Cited

Baehr, Jason S. 2011. *The Inquiring Mind: On Intellectual Virtues and Virtue Epistemology.* Oxford: Oxford University Press.

Basso, Keith H. 1979. *Portraits of "The Whiteman": Linguistic Play and Cultural Symbols among the Western Apache.* Cambridge: Cambridge University Press, 1979. https://search.library.wisc.edu/catalog/999504365302121.

Churchill, Ward. 1998. *Fantasies of the Master Race: Literature, Cinema, and the Colonization of American Indians.* San Francisco: City Lights Books.

Comas-Díaz, Lillian. 2000. "An Ethnopolitical Approach to Working with People of Color." *American Psychologist* 55(11): 1319–1325. https://doi.org/10.1037/0003-066X.55.11.1319.

Cruikshank, Julie. 2001. "Oral History, Narrative Strategies, and Native American Historiography: Perspectives from the Yukon Territory, Canada." In Clearing a Path: Theorizing the Past in Native American Studies, ed. Nancy Shoemaker (pp. 3–28). New York: Routledge.

Dancy, T. Elon, Kirsten T. Edwards, and James Earl Davis. 2018. "Historically White Universities and Plantation Politics: Anti-Blackness and Higher Education in the Black Lives Matter Era." *Urban Education* 53(2): 176–195. https://doi.org/10.1177/0042085918754328.

Deloria, Vine. 1988. *Custer Died for Your Sins: An Indian Manifesto.* Norman: University of Oklahoma Press.

Dei, George J. Sefa. 2006. "Introduction: Mapping the Terrain: Towards a New Politics of Resistance." In Anti-Colonialism and Education: The Politics of Resistance, ed. George J. Sefi Dei and Arlo Kempf (pp. ix–x). Boston, MA: Sense Publishers.

100 THE VIRTUE OF OPEN-MINDEDNESS

Grosfoguel, Ramón. 2007. "The Epistemic Decolonial Turn: Beyond Political-Economy Paradigms." *Cultural Studies* 21(2–3): 211–223. https://doi.org/10.1080/09502380601162514.

Hare, William. 1979. *Open-Mindedness and Education.* Montreal: McGill-Queen's University Press. http://site.ebrary.com/id/10175984.

Jackson, Rachel C. 2017. "Resisting Relocation: Placing Leadership on Decolonized Indigenous Landscapes." *College English* 79(5): 495–511.

Moane, Geraldine. 1999. *Gender and Colonialism: A Psychological Analysis of Oppression and Liberation.* Basingstoke: Palgrave Macmillan. http://site.ebrary.com/id/10606847.

Nandy, Ashis. 2009. *The Intimate Enemy: Loss and Recovery of Self under Colonialism,* 2nd ed., 4th impr. Oxford India Paperbacks. New Delhi: Oxford University Press.

Riggs, Wayne. 2010. "Open-Mindedness." *Metaphilosophy* 41(1–2): 172–188. https://doi.org/10.1111/j.1467-9973.2009.01625.x.

Smith, Linda Tuhiwai. 2013. *Decolonizing Methodologies: Research and Indigenous Peoples.* London: Zed Books; Distributed in the USA exclusively by St. Martin's Press.

Toth, Christie. 2016. "Seeing Settler Colonialism." *College English* 78(5): 496–510.

Vizenor, Gerald Robert, ed. 1993. *Narrative Chance: Postmodern Discourse on Native American Indian Literatures.* American Indian Literature and Critical Studies Series 8. Norman: University of Oklahoma Press.

Wolfe, Patrick. 2006. "Settler Colonialism and the Elimination of the Native." *Journal of Genocide Research* 8(4): 387–409. https://doi.org/10.1080/146235 20601056240.

4

Free Speech and Challenges to Open-Mindedness in Higher Education

Emily Robertson

In 1985 William Hare published his now classic *In Defense of Open-mindedness*.[1] In re-reading the book, I was struck by its contemporary relevance. The differences in context between 1985 and today, however, require a reconsideration of some of the issues Hare raised, as well as new defenses. On the one hand, open-mindedness seems crucially important but in short supply in the current political environment. On the other hand, the concept of open-mindedness has been adopted by some on the political right who are actually undermining truth and expertise in the public mind, while open-mindedness is seemingly rejected by its traditional allies, the liberal left, in their efforts to support members of oppressed groups subject to hate speech. The traditional connections between open-mindedness and free speech and their importance to democracy and the public sphere need to be rethought.

1 Preliminaries

There are different accounts of open-mindedness in the philosophical literature. Hare describes open-mindedness as involving, at its core, being both willing and able "to revise and reconsider one's views ... in light of evidence and argument."[2] Baehr expands this account: "An open-minded person is characteristically (a) willing and

Emily Robertson, *Free Speech and Challenges to Open-Mindedness in Higher Education* In: *The Virtue of Open-Mindedness and Perspective*. Edited by: Wayne D. Riggs, Oxford University Press. © Oxford University Press 2025. DOI: 10.1093/9780190080723.003.0005

102   THE VIRTUE OF OPEN-MINDEDNESS

(within limits) able (b) to transcend a default cognitive standpoint (c) in order to take up or take seriously the merits of (d) a distinct cognitive standpoint."[3] An important point that I think Baehr gets right in this condition is his emphasis on "cognitive standpoint" as the subject of open-mindedness. If I believe that the faculty meeting is on Wednesday and my chair tells me it's on Thursday, I'm not demonstrating my open-mindedness when I change my mind. The stakes are not high enough. Whatever a cognitive standpoint is, it's an epistemic unit bigger than a stand-alone fact, something akin to what Riggs calls a "perspective," an interrelated set of mutually reinforcing representations that figure in our explanations and understanding of some aspect of the world.[4]

Baehr acknowledges that the preceding account, however, is not sufficient for defining open-mindedness as an intellectual *virtue*. The virtuously open-minded person will exercise judgment about when to consider the merits of a different cognitive standpoint. Virtuous agents will consider the alternatives only when they have reason to believe that doing so may be truth conducive. No one should, for example, be open-minded about whether slavery is wrong. Seriously considering whether slavery is good social practice is not truth conducive.[5]

As an educational philosopher, I am interested in when open-mindedness is virtuous and how we might teach students to become virtuously open-minded. Using Aristotle's schema for moral virtues, open-mindedness as a virtue can be construed as a mean between two extremes. A deficit of open-mindedness is closed-mindedness, which involves a characteristic imperviousness to alternative views. An excess of open-mindedness is captured by Michael Frayn's description of Haugh, a character in his novella *The Tin Men*: "But above all, Haugh had an open mind. It was open at the front, and it was open at the back. Opinions, beliefs, philosophies entered, sojourned briefly, and were pushed out at the other end by the press of incoming convictions and systems."[6] Being properly open-minded, then, requires hitting the mean, that is, being neither impervious to other perspectives nor willing to seriously entertain any idea one encounters however bad.

A second background assumption in this chapter concerns how teachers can promote open-mindedness. As Riggs says, "Paradigm cases of open-mindedness tend to involve the ability and willingness

FREE SPEECH AND CHALLENGES 103

of one person to consider fully and conscientiously the viewpoint of someone else with whom they initially disagree, in other words, to take seriously the possibility that they are wrong."[7] Teachers typically seek to encourage such an outlook by engaging students in discussions of controversial issues.[8] Teaching students to listen respectfully to others with whom they initially disagree and reevaluating their own positions in light of such discussions is what teachers attempt to model and teach. Thus teaching controversial issues is taken to be conducive to the development of open-mindedness.

When an issue is legitimately regarded as controversial is contentious. The main current candidates for criteria to determine which issues are controversial are the "epistemic criterion"[9] and the "politically authentic criterion"[10] For the former, the paradigm case of a controversial issue is one where informed people can reasonably disagree, there being multiple rational positions that can be held on the question. For the latter, whether an issue is controversial depends on the current political and social context. Issues are controversial "when they have traction in the public sphere, appearing on ballots, in courts, within political platforms, in legislative chambers, and as part of political movements."[11] While these criteria may often point to the same issues, there are cases where they diverge. The relationship between vaccines and autism persisted in social movements and court cases long after valid scientific studies had shown no effect, for example. Today anthropogenic global climate change remains a politically divisive issue although climate scientists are in near universal agreement that it is real. The claim that immigrants commit crimes in greater numbers than native-born citizens continues to animate some political parties' agendas in immigration debates despite data to the contrary. While these claims may look like simple statements of scientific fact, not the perspectives invoked in the definition of open-mindedness, they are typically embedded in larger political standpoints that make them desirable or plausible to their advocates. Changing a person's mind requires addressing these background perspectives as well as the more limited statement of fact.

Since open-mindedness aims at truth, the epistemic criterion would seem to be the correct criterion for judging when one should maintain a stance of open-mindedness toward a controversial issue.

104 THE VIRTUE OF OPEN-MINDEDNESS

Nevertheless, the political criterion may appear to be the right standard for determining when moral and political issues are controversial. Here, it is sometimes said, we should maintain an open-minded stance and "teach the controversies" by presenting all sides fairly and let the students decide what to believe, since there are no "experts" to guide us. Sometimes this is clearly the appropriate stance. But it cannot be the case that all moral issues are controversial, that is, that there is no clear truth of the matter in all cases. Bullying is wrong even if there remain genuine controversies about what counts as bullying. For teachers, the even-handed approach can land them in hot water when each side believes strongly in the truth or rightness of its own position, thus holding that the other side is ignorant, radically mistaken, or morally corrupt. In such cases, teachers who treat "the other side" as having something to be said for it will generate outrage among some community members. What counts as being open-minded for some will constitute immorality or blatant political bias for others. These facts explain why, despite a lot of lip service to teaching controversial issues in public schools, not a lot of it actually goes on.[12]

2 Open-Mindedness: Right versus Left

One challenge to open-mindedness presented by Hare is that "in some sorts of cases, the open-minded consideration of views must necessarily frustrate the pursuit of truth, and introduce an element of distortion." Hare continues, we may hold "'as a matter of moral conviction, that certain topics should not even be discussed.' The problem which this fact generates is not that in discussing an issue we may be less than fair to a particular point of view, but that in discussing it at all one rides rough-shod over the views of some."[13] It appears that here Hare points to two seemingly different issues in one discussion. The idea that "open-minded consideration of views must necessarily frustrate the pursuit of truth" is an especially serious challenge. The second claim that discussion of alternative viewpoints may ride "rough-shod over the views of some" and hence that "as a moral matter certain topics should not be discussed" seems to be a different point, although Hare presents it as an example of the first. The first issue concerns the

FREE SPEECH AND CHALLENGES 105

truth of the matter, while the second involves sensitivity to when an interlocutor's moral sensibilities may be offended. I will consider these challenges independently.

Open-mindedness is typically thought of as a virtue that supports liberal democracy along with reasonableness and support for free speech, among others. From that point of view, one of the many strange aspects of today's political discourse is the usurping of open-mindedness along with free speech by the conservative right. In 2011, the Board of Education of the Los Alamitos School District voted to require that teachers offer "multiple perspectives" on the science of global warming.[14] The claim that teachers should be "open-minded" about the human contribution to climate change or evolution and teach alternative points of view, for example, supports the conservative claims against these views by claiming that they are open questions, i.e., that they are ones where reasonable disagreement is possible. Those who protest are viewed as not being open-minded. Yet in such cases to be willing to engage in discussion is already to concede the conservative claim, i.e., that global warming is controversial and hence not settled fact.

As Hare and Baehr suggest, judging that an issue is controversial and deserves an open-minded treatment depends on the current state of knowledge. When the overwhelming majority of climate scientists hold that humans do significantly contribute to global warming, students have a right to know what the best science says. The teachers' freedom to teach is the flip side of students' right to know. To teach students that anthropogenic global warming is genuinely controversial is to seriously mislead them: treating this issue as controversial implies that the existence of global warming (or the human contribution to it) is undecided when actually the scientific facts are clear.[15] This strategy, then, undermines the truth by treating an issue as open to debate when it is not. Here I side with the epistemic criterion for when an issue is controversial.[16]

Nevertheless, teachers can put their careers at risk in some areas of the country by teaching scientifically well-validated knowledge. Some argue that students should be made aware of the reasons offered on both sides of the issue and allowed to draw their own conclusions, the "open-minded" strategy of teaching the controversies.[17] However, in

106   THE VIRTUE OF OPEN-MINDEDNESS

cases such as the human contribution to global warming it's not possible for the students or even their teachers to fully appreciate and evaluate the evidence. The science involved in global warming and its causes are complex. Evaluating the facts requires understanding computer modeling and the way these predictive models are developed and tested on the basis of extensive observational data and experimental findings. While students (and their teachers) can hope to achieve some understanding, they will not be in a position to evaluate the experts' data and findings themselves.

Some might accuse teachers who hold that the human contribution to climate change is not open to dispute have become closed-minded. Hare considers the claim that open-mindedness is incompatible with commitment. In reply, he says: "Open-mindedness is exercised critically, and will itself demand that certain ideas be resisted." "Commitment and closed-mindedness" are not the same thing.[18] One can continue to have the virtue of open-mindedness while judging that a particular issue is settled. Of course, if one does have the virtue, one would be willing to reconsider if new evidence emerges that suggests it is appropriate to rethink the issue. But absent such evidence, commitment is reasonable. Thus teachers who resist being "open-minded" about climate change are not in fact guilty as charged. As Baehr says, having the *virtue* of open-mindedness depends on whether considering the alternative position is more likely to allow one to discover the truth. In this case, teaching students to consider the alternative is more likely to lead them astray than to convey the truth of the matter.

In the days of "alternative facts" and allegedly "fake news," some members of the public do not hold expertise in high regard or respect the epistemic division of labor. Respect for teachers as purveyors of expert knowledge is similarly weak. The ability to resist belief in anthropogenic global warming despite overwhelming scientific evidence to the contrary is abetted by epistemic deficiencies of our social and political environment. A politically balkanized media make it possible for deniers to find "facts" that accord with their views. Even the mainstream, supposedly responsible, media gin up controversy where there is none by inappropriate applications of a fairness doctrine that makes them believe they must give due respect to the "opposition." Thus achieving the goal of teaching students when an open-minded

FREE SPEECH AND CHALLENGES 107

approach to issues is warranted depends on the soundness of our epistemic institutions.

Decisions about when to regard an issue as settled, and hence to hold that "teaching the controversy" is not the right strategy, becomes more difficult when moral or political issues are at stake where there are no agreed upon-experts to guide us. Just as in certain contexts conservatives champion open-mindedness and free speech, contrary to previous script, so too do some on the political left appear to reject these virtues when views are regarded as denigrating oppressed groups. Milo Yiannopoulos, former editor of Breitbart News, holds some views in common with neo-Nazis, white supremacists, and the alt-right. Despite being gay, he regards homosexuality as a sin. He was banned from Twitter for instigating a campaign of racial harassment and has been accused of endorsing pedophilia (which he denies). He has argued that women are made "crazy" by birth control and decried women being in the military. In short, he has given evidence through his writings of being a white supremacist, as well as racist, homophobic, and misogynist. Yiannopoulos has been an invited speaker at several university campuses where he has been confronted by sometimes violent student protests, most notably at the University of California at Berkeley. In the aftermath, President Trump criticized Berkeley for not supporting free speech.[19]

Not all speech or action judged to be offensive rises to Yiannopoulos's level of provocation. Some Yale students were offended by criticism of a request that students avoid offensive Halloween costumes and some Emory students were upset by "Trump 2016" signs chalked on sidewalks.[20] Wendy Hyman, an Oberlin associate professor of English, in a *New Yorker* interview, remarks that her generation (college students in the 1980s) "protested against Tipper Gore for wanting to put warning labels on records. 'My students want warning labels on class content, and I feel—I don't even know how to articulate it,' she said. 'Part of me feels that my leftist students are doing the right wing's job for it'"[21] A Pew Research poll found that 40 percent of millennials think the government should be able to regulate some forms of offensive speech. This is compared with 20 percent of baby boomers.[22] Reasons for this transformation include differences in the political realities students face. In the 1960s, students endorsed

108 THE VIRTUE OF OPEN-MINDEDNESS

free speech in light of university administrators' attempts to suppress anti-war protests, for example. The greater diversity of today's college campuses makes students more aware than earlier generations of the ways in which offensive speech creates hostile learning environments for targeted students. We now know that "names" do "hurt," not merely victims' feelings but also their ability to do their jobs, to participate in educational experiences, and their psychological and physical well-being.[23]

According to conservative criticism of current campus politics, "The ultimate aim, it seems, is to turn campuses into 'safe spaces' where young adults are shielded from words and ideas that make some un-comfortable."[24] Campuses that respond to student protests positively are accused of furthering intellectual homogeneity on campus, a state of affairs that makes open-mindedness more difficult because diverse views are not represented for students to encounter. The Foundation for Individual Rights in Education (FIRE) rates campuses on their commitments to free speech and legally supports students and faculty who believe that their views have been suppressed.

But while it's easy to make college students' claims look overblown by citing examples of overreach that are easy to condemn (physical violence, for example), the issues they're confronting are real and not easily solved. As campuses (and society at large) have become more committed to including people previously marginalized by race, reli-gion, class, gender, disability, sexual orientation, and gender identity, the extent of social injustices committed within all our institutions has become more apparent. How can universities combine their commit-ment to open-mindedness, free speech, and academic freedom with their desire to be inclusive and welcoming to all students? Is it possible to draw distinctions between speech that must be permitted, even if it's offensive to some, and speech and opinions that demean some groups of students and harm their ability to be part of the learning community and hence should be discouraged? Or should every view be open to debate in the interest of free speech and open-mindedness?

Jeremy Waldron has proposed that a distinction can be drawn be-tween speech that diminishes the dignity of some groups of citizens and speech that offends them.[25] Waldron supports laws against hate speech in the former, but not the latter, cases. (Waldron develops a

FREE SPEECH AND CHALLENGES   109

composite definition of "hate speech" based on hate speech laws in Canada, Denmark, Germany, and New Zealand: hate speech is "the use of words which are deliberately abusive and/or insulting and/or threatening and/or demeaning directed at members of vulnerable minorities, calculated to stir up hatred against them.")[26] Dignity, says Waldron, is an objective social fact about a person's standing in society. An attack on the dignity of a social group diminishes its members' standing as equal citizens entitled to justice before the law. Attacks on dignity allege that members of a particular group, in virtue of their ascriptive characteristics, are not entitled to "being treated as members of society in good standing." Being offended, on the other hand, is a subjective state, "aspects of feeling, including hurt, shock, and anger."[27] Likely people whose dignity is assaulted will be offended as well, but not all offensive speech involves an attack on dignity. Caricatures of Jews as hook-nosed, greedy bankers are an affront to dignity, given the history and use of those images. They indicate that Jews are less than human and should be accorded a lesser status in society. Wearing "Make America Great Again" hats may offend some immigrant groups, for example, but it does not necessarily diminish the dignity of members of these groups as human beings.

Is this an example of a case where "open-minded" debate, with the anti-Semite, for example, may, as Hare's critic argued, "necessarily frustrate the pursuit of truth, and introduce an element of distortion" in a way similar to that of debating climate change? I think it can be argued that it does. Waldron proposes that, in a well-ordered society, dignity is a good that each citizen implicitly provides to the others by refraining from actions that would undermine it. Hate speech laws enforce this good in countries that have them. To debate, for example, whether Jews are greedy bankers who control the world's money supply by treating it as a proposition up for grabs "is exactly what the speech in question aims for." It signals to members of vulnerable groups that they cannot take for granted the support of their fellow citizens, that there may be more people who feel the same way as the anti-Semites than they thought. They can no longer be certain that the society overall implicitly acknowledges their dignity. For that reason, Waldron argues, it may not be a bad thing to drive such speech underground.[28]

110 THE VIRTUE OF OPEN-MINDEDNESS

Hare's second claim, that discussion of alternative viewpoints may ride "rough-shod over the views of some" and hence that "as a moral matter certain topics should not be discussed" may be an example of Waldron's second category of insults that he argues should not be protected by hate speech laws. Some liberal-left demands to shut down conversation may fall into this category. "Trump 2016" signs chalked on university sidewalks may well be offensive to those who believe Trump is a racist and deplore his policies, but such signs do not clearly demean the dignity of minority racial groups. More challenging to classify are speakers such as Charles Murray, who holds that genetic differences are a major part of the differences in IQ across races (Blacks having lower IQs than whites) and that these differences are a determinant in economic and social differences across races. Students have protested his invitations to speak at their campuses, including Harvard and Middlebury, even when the topic was not about race. The protesters argue that his views are racist and scientifically invalid (as numerous scholars have pointed out) and have no place on college campuses. Others argue that the proper stance is to counter his views with argument if students believe he is wrong, but that he has a right to speak and be heard by those who invited him. Of course, no one has a right to be given a platform to speech at a college or university. Typically, invitations are given by a wide range of organizations including academic departments and student organizations. Once issued, to rescind the invitation on the basis of the speaker's perspective on fraught issues risks infringing their free speech rights. More important in the university context, it risks diminishing the opportunity for students to hear from the speaker. It is not done lightly. Waldron acknowledges that the distinction between when dignity is at stake and when affronts are simply matters of insult is not always easy to make, but here "more speech" seems likely the correct answer.

3   Free Speech, Open-Mindedness, and Hate Speech

Advocates of free speech argue that constraints cannot be placed on the content of adult speech within public institutions and hence that regulations against hate speech are inappropriate. The free speech

FREE SPEECH AND CHALLENGES 111

clause of the First Amendment reads: "Congress shall make no law . . . abridging the freedom of speech." This clause has been interpreted to mean, in the words of Justice Thurgood Marshall, that

> government has no power to restrict expression because of its message, its ideas, its subject matter, or its content. . . . [O]ur people are guaranteed the right to express any thought, free from government censorship. . . . Any restriction on expressive activity because of its content would completely undercut the 'profound national commitment to the principle that debate on public issues should be uninhibited, robust, and wide-open.' "[29]

As Marshall's words make plain, the free speech principle applies only to censorship by the government. One is not free to criticize a private employer, for example, without being subject to discipline by appealing to the First Amendment. Thus only public colleges and universities cannot restrict speech covered by the First Amendment, although if private schools intend to enforce speech codes, they must make their policies plain before students enroll (and they have to abide by any unchallenged state laws that may prohibit hate speech codes).

There are numerous limitations on free speech in the United States: "conspiracy; defamation and libel; copyright; plagiarism; official secrets; misleading advertising, words of threat."[30] Nevertheless, the United States does not have laws against hate speech, unlike many other countries. Canada, for example, declares as an "indictable offense" promoting hatred (except in private conversation) against "any section of the public distinguished by colour, race, religion, national or ethnic origin, age, sex, sexual orientation, gender identity or expression, or mental or physical disability."[31] Some of the existing restrictions to the First Amendment may look promising as ways of limiting hate speech, such as defamation and libel and threatening words. The history of jurisprudence in this area is too complex to review here, but the requirements for proving any of these offenses with respect to hate speech has been difficult. Proving defamation or libel requires that specific individuals be targeted, not groups (as in so-called "group libel"). "True threats" occur when the speaker manifests a serious intent to physically harm an individual or group such that

112   THE VIRTUE OF OPEN-MINDEDNESS

their words would make a reasonable person fear for their safety. That the person or persons targeted are insulted or fearful is not enough. While protections against workplace harassment have been extended to students, these harms apply only when harassment of specific individuals makes it impossible for them to benefit from or participate in their own education or the educational activities of the institution. In short, it is very difficult to prosecute hate speech in the United States.[32] All hate speech codes adopted by universities and challenged in court have been declared unconstitutional to date.[33]

Why protect bigoted speech? What are the values or rights that strong commitments to free speech protect? If the government can forbid the content of speech it thinks inappropriate, then we empower the government (or the university administration) to determine what speech is forbidden. And that is dangerous to democracy, defenders of free speech hold. Who's to say that such power will not be used in the future, as it has in the past, to silence unpopular but just causes? Further, some argue that maintaining democratic government requires it. In a democracy, the people decide for themselves which candidates for public office should be chosen. Full information and expression of interests are required for this process to work properly. Further, the search for truth requires an open marketplace of ideas in which the true ones will ultimately prevail over false ones. Or, at least, the truth is less likely to prevail under censorship where it can be suppressed by the government. Truth is important for the creation of knowledge not only in scientific realms but also in social and political ideas if individuals and collectives are to be able to craft ways of life that are good for them.[34] Open-mindedness is of little benefit if the public is prohibited from learning what options are genuine alternatives to its current point of view. And free speech is more likely to be endorsed by those who are open to new ideas, i.e., those who are open-minded.[35]

If we are persuaded by these claims, how should universities deal with hate speech? The American Civil Liberties Union holds that where "racist, misogynist, homophobic, and transphobic speech is concerned, . . . more speech—not less—is the answer most consistent with our constitutional values."[36] Those who argue that free speech should include hate speech argue that it is better to have such views out in the open where they can be confronted. Thomas Jefferson,

FREE SPEECH AND CHALLENGES 113

upon founding the University of Virginia, said: "This institution will be based on the illimitable freedom of the human mind. For here we are not afraid to follow truth wherever it may lead, nor to tolerate any error so long as reason is left free to combat it."[37] More recently, Barack Obama in a Rutgers graduation speech, said, "Don't feel like you got to shut your ears off because you're too fragile and somebody might offend your sensibilities. Go at them if they're not making any sense. Use your logic and reason and words."[38]

Are we so sure in these days of Facebook, Twitter trolls, and "fake news" that reason and truth really will prevail against hate speech? Is it possible that allowing the Milo Yiannopouloses of this world to speak in public settings degrades the public good Waldron described of implicitly supporting the dignity of all citizens? Do such speakers bring others who share those views out in the open where they can form alliances rather than be refuted? Given the current proliferation of speech in combination with its siloing, can arguments really be confronted with opposing views?

It seems likely that no single speaking engagement can undermine some group's humanity, but when such events are part of a persistent pattern, dignity can be challenged. Given the history of race in America, there is no doubt that racial insults are not isolated events in the life of minority group members. "Each act (of racist speech) seems harmless but . . . in combination with others, crushes the spirits of victims while creating culture at odds with our national values."[39] An individual event may seem trivial or ambiguous (e.g., blackface as part of a Halloween costume depicting an African American) to white people who often see only the most egregious expressions of racism through social media. But for African Americans who constantly experience microaggressions as well more substantial expressions of racism, the individual event is part of long-standing patterns of racialized experience that generates firsthand knowledge of how racism works in this country. The guilt or innocence of a student who wore black-face is not the whole story.[40]

The recommendation to "confront and counter offensive speech" is where debating controversial issues and exhortations to open-mindedness enter the picture. But our prior discussion suggests that care is needed in how these "debates" are framed. If we adopt a political

114 THE VIRTUE OF OPEN-MINDEDNESS

definition of "controversial issues," then these issues are truly controversial and discussion should treat them as genuinely open questions where open-mindedness is required. If, however, we adopt an epistemic definition of when an issue is controversial, commitment is appropriate: the issue is not controversial and someone who takes that position is not being closed-minded. Since willingness to entertain the claim if evidence changes is sufficient for open-mindedness, we are not required to treat such issues as genuinely open. Here our response becomes less a matter of debate and more a matter of "talking back."[41]

It is important to clearly distinguish between the virtue of open-mindedness, which is truth oriented, and the political principle of free speech, which is not necessarily truth oriented (unless you accept the theory of the marketplace of ideas, whose truth, especially these days, is doubtful). In reading Rebecca Taylor's account of Charles Murray's visit to Middlebury College in 2017,[42] for example, I was struck by some faculty's refusal to acknowledge the element of judgment in open-mindedness. "A good education produces modesty with respect to our own intellectual powers and opinions as well as openness to considering contrary views." Students should not attempt to "limit acceptable questions for discussion and debate." Yes, we ought to consider contrary views if we're open-minded, but not, as some students rightly insisted, when those views are clearly false:

> By elevating bigotry and engaging with it in open debate under the misguided view that all ideas must be respected, we risk elevating biased opinions with no solid, factual foundation into the realm of 'knowledge' and affirming the unconscious biases many hold. . . . If we hold that the contest of clashing viewpoints is the only way to solidify knowledge, it naturally follows that we have a responsibility to articulate some parameters for which viewpoints are worthy of such a process.[43]

Thus the students are right when they protest being asked to seriously consider the inferiority of African Americans as portrayed in Murray's much debunked *Bell Curve* (although it was actually his more recent book, *Coming Apart*, that he was asked to discuss at Middlebury). We are not required to consider clearly false views in order to be

FREE SPEECH AND CHALLENGES 115

open-minded. And members of a university community have no obligation to entertain such views. Indeed, they have an obligation to debunk them.

The issue in Murray's case isn't about the need to be open-minded about his findings in the *Bell Curve* (one needn't be given that it's been roundly rebuffed by those in a position to know) but rather whether the students ought to accord him free speech once invited. As things currently stand in the law, the answer is likely yes. But I read the students as challenging that finding. Free speech is not absolute even now. Should it exclude various forms of hate speech, as some Western democracies do? And, if so, on what grounds? The idea that all views should be respected and all contributions valued, that all talk should proceed as if in a deliberative forum that honors ideal speech, is a mistake. As John Palfrey writes in *Safe Spaces, Brave Spaces*: "Our system of governance must also call for a point at which the tolerant may become intolerant of intolerance. The intolerant should not be able to dominate merely by calling on the tolerant to tolerate their intolerance. The hard problem of hate speech is where that line—between the political speech we must tolerate, no matter how obnoxious, and the hate speech we should not tolerate—is drawn."[44]

In the present political climate, it is clear that laws against hate speech are not going to be passed in the United States any time soon. How, then, should we deal with hate speech on college campuses and elsewhere? What can universities do? A Middlebury professor, in the wake of sometimes violent protests over Murray's invitation to speak, said that the college had done a poor job of teaching their students the arguments for free speech. If this is true, then we should remedy the situation. Students should know that free speech has sometimes protected minorities advocating social justice (but also sometimes not).[45] But we should also acknowledge that those attacked by hate speech are the ones who suffer harm from it, not usually the defenders of free speech. We should engage in honest arguments about the alleged values of free speech. It goes without saying that one of the benefits of university education is the chance to expand one's perspectives beyond those of one's communities of birth. Such expansion is part of the opportunity to develop greater open-mindedness. But those who are targets of hate rarely are unaware of those hateful views. The empirical

116 THE VIRTUE OF OPEN-MINDEDNESS

claim that truth will out in the marketplace of ideas must be balanced with evidence that hate speech emboldens others who share the same views to make themselves known and to band together. Commitment to a view that is rationally supported and unwillingness to engage in open-minded consideration of a view that denigrates those suffering from oppression is not the same as closed-mindedness. If hate speech must be tolerated on free speech grounds, this is not because the ideas deserve an open-minded hearing.

What forms of social pressure can we bring to bear that makes it clear that such views are not welcome here? Appropriate institutional actions against hate speech include increasing the diversity of faculty, students, and administrators and teaching students about the history of bigotry, including microaggressions. Even if codes against hate speech whose violations are punishable are not permitted, statements of the community's expectations of its members are permitted. Students need training in how to support those who are targets of hate speech as well as how to confront those who express hate, when it can be done safely. When the transgressors are well-meaning but uninformed, tensions can be diffused by a strategy that Loretta J. Ross terms "calling them in" rather than "calling them out." Instead of publicly shaming people, Ross recommends speaking to them privately and with respect.[46]

Democracy may be more fragile than we think. Ironically, the issue of the limits of free speech is well worth debating. College students have opened the door to this discussion. Instead of demeaning them, let us have an open mind.

Acknowledgment: I am indebted to Barbara Applebaum, Randall Curren, William Hare, and Rebecca Taylor for written comments on earlier drafts of this chapter and to the participants of the Conference on Open-mindedness at the University of Oklahoma's Center for Human Flourishing for discussion of the first draft of this chapter.

Notes

1. William Hare, *In Defense of Open-mindedness* (Montreal: McGill-Queen's University Press, 1985).
2. William Hare, *Open-mindedness and Education* (Montreal: McGill-Queen's University Press, 1979), x, 8, 9.
3. Jason Baehr, *The Inquiring Mind* (Oxford: Oxford University Press, 2011), 152. Of course, whatever perspective is open to critical examination, there is always a

FREE SPEECH AND CHALLENGES 117

currently unexamined, taken-for-granted background or else there would be no resources for undertaking the examination. See Rockey Robbins in this volume for further explication of this point.

4. Wayne Riggs, "Open-Mindedness, Insight, and Understanding," in *Intellectual Virtues and Education: Essays in Applied Virtue Epistemology*, ed. Jason Baehr (p. 19) (New York: Routledge, 2016).

5. The concern for truth belongs to an epistemic conception of open-mindedness. Some have suggested that open-mindedness can be thought of as a moral virtue where truth might not be the appropriate aim. See Yujia Song, "The Moral Virtue of Open-Mindedness," *Canadian Journal of Philosophy* 48(1):1–20. This article focuses on the epistemic conception, if there is an alternative moral conception. Further, even the epistemic conception might involve ends other than truth, such as understanding or the expansion of possibilities (as when a person who had thought of poetry as necessarily involving rhyme or meter comes to see blank verse as poetry). See Baehr, *The Inquiring Mind*, 147. See also Susan Verducci, "The Arts and Open-Mindedness," *Educational Theory* 69(4): 495–401.

6. Michael Frayn, *The Tin Men* (London: Fontana Paperbacks, 1966), 66.

7. Riggs, "Open-Mindedness," 22.

8. For a fuller exposition of this claim, see Jon Zimmerman and Emily Robertson, *The Case for Contention: Teaching Controversial Issues in American Schools* (Chicago: University of Chicago Press, 2017).

9. R. F. Dearden, "Controversial Issues in the Curriculum," *Journal of Curriculum Studies* 13: 37–44; Michael Hand, "What Should We Teach as Controversial? A Defense of the Epistemic Criterion," *Educational Theory* 58: 213–228.

10. Diana E. Hess and Paula McAvoy, *The Political Classroom: Evidence and Ethics in the Democratic Classroom* (New York: Routledge, 2015), 168–169.

11. Hess and McAvoy, *The Political Classroom*.

12. See Zimmerman and Robertson, "Historical Reflections," 8–43.

13. Hare, *In Defense of Open-mindedness*, 5. The embedded quotation is from Geoffrey Warnock, "Education and Pluralism: What Sort of Problems?" *Oxford Review of Education* 1(2): 95.

14. Leo Hickman, "US School Board Teaches 'the Controversy' on Global Warming," *The Guardian*, May 17, 2011.

15. For a similar argument concerning "teaching the controversies" with respect to evolution and intelligent design, see Eugenie C. Scott, "What's Wrong with the 'Teach the Controversy' Slogan?" *McGill Journal of Education* 4(2): 307–315.

16. For a possible objection to this view, see John Lambie, *How to Be Critically Open-Minded: A Psychological and Historical Analysis* (Cambridge: Palgrave Macmillan, 2014). Lambie appears to criticize the view that open-mindedness is not incompatible with commitment in his account of "critical open-mindedness." He criticizes Aristotle's position that we should not examine every claim by reason, since some things "admit of no doubt." Lambie says that "critical open-mindedness is a kind of 'permanent revolution' of thought in which nothing is ever fixed or justified, criticism is all pervasive, and assent to a belief is always provisional" (p. 192). However, as far as I can tell, this claim seems to amount to the same position as Hare's that one would be willing to reconsider if new relevant evidence became available. For example, Lambie says that "what the critically open-minded person means when he or she asserts things" is what Scheffler means when he says that "there is a horse; and I recognize the possibility that the statement might be withdrawn under other circumstances than those now prevailing" (cited in Lambie, *How to Be Critically Open-minded*, 189).

118   THE VIRTUE OF OPEN-MINDEDNESS

17. Bryan R. Warnick and D. Spencer Smith, "The Controversy over Controversies: A Plea for Flexibility and for 'Soft-Directive' Teaching," *Educational Theory* 64(3): 227–244.
18. Hare, *In Defense of Open-mindedness,* 83. See also Hare, *Open-mindedness and Education,* 29–45, for an extended discussion of the issue of commitment and open-mindedness.
19. "Milo Yiannopoulos," Wikipedia, https://en.wikipedia.org/wiki/Milo_Yiannopoulos, accessed September 12, 2018.
20. I'm not suggesting that these students had no grounds for complaint, but that the actions in these cases were not as egregious as Yiannopoulos's claims. The situation at Emory in particular was more complex than is typically reported in the media. See https://www.newsweek.com/emory-trump-chalk-protests-440618 for a more nuanced discussion of this event.
21. Nathan Heller, "The Big Uneasy: What's Roiling the Liberal Arts Campus," *New Yorker* 92(16), https://www.newyorker.com/magazine/2016/05/30/the-new-activism-of-liberal-arts-colleges.
22. Clay Routledge, "Millennials Are Wary of Freedom," *New York Times; Sunday Review,* October 14, 2017, https://www.nytimes.com/2017/10/14/opinion/sunday/millennials-freedom-fear.html, accessed September 12, 2018.
23. Richard Delgado and Jean Stefancic, *Must We Defend Nazis? Hate Speech, Pornography and the New First Amendment* (New York: New York University Press, 1997), 4–10.
24. Greg Lukianoff and Jonathan Haidt, "The Coddling of the American Mind," *The Atlantic,* September 2015. https://www.theatlantic.com/magazine/archive/2015/09/the-coddling-of-the-american-mind/399356/, accessed September 11, 2018.
25. For another account of how to apply Waldron's distinctions to university issues of free speech, see Sigal R. Ben-Porath, *Free Speech on Campus* (Philadelphia: University of Pennsylvania Press, 2017). See also Michele Moody-Adams's use of the distinction in her account of academic freedom: "Is There a 'Safe Space' for Academic Freedom?" in *Academic Freedom,* ed. Jennifer Lackey (pp. 36–61) (Oxford: Oxford University Press, 2018).
26. Jeremy Waldron, *The Harm in Hate Speech* (Cambridge, MA: Harvard University Press, 2012), 8–9.
27. Waldron, *The Harm in Hate Speech,* 106.
28. Waldron, *The Harm in Hate Speech,* 95–96.
29. *Police Dept. of Chicago v. Mosley,* 408 U.S. 92 (1972).
30. Delgado and Stefancic, *Must We Defend Nazis?,* 63.
31. *Criminal Code of Canada,* Section 319(2).
32. Erwin Chemerinsky and Howard Gillman, *Free Speech on Campus* (New Haven, CT: Yale University Press, 2017), Chap. 5.
33. For a helpful history of hate speech legislation, see Erik Bleich, "The Rise of Hate Speech and Hate Crime Laws in Liberal Democracies," *Journal of Ethnic and Migration Studies* 37(6): 917–934. See also Chemerinsky and Gillman, *Free Speech on Campus.*
34. Caleb Yong, "Does Freedom of Speech Include Hate Speech?" *Res Publica* 17(4): 385–403.
35. Some argue that a commitment to free speech whatever the content is especially important for academic freedom in universities. Academic freedom, however, is bounded by academic norms of competence and ethical behavior whereas free speech is not limited by these conditions. See Chemerinsky and Gillman, *Free Speech on Campus,* Chap. 3.
36. ACLU, "Free Speech on Campus," obtained from aclu.org on August 15, 2018.
37. As quoted in Lukianoff and Haidt, "The Coddling of the American Mind."

FREE SPEECH AND CHALLENGES   119

38. As quoted in Heller, "The Big Uneasy."
39. Delgado and Stefancic, *Must We Defend Nazis?* 69.
40. See Doug Glanville, "Was I Racially Taunted?" *New York Times*, May 19, 2019, *Sunday Review*, 2.
41. Galil Ablow, "Talking Back to Hate Speech, Explained," billmoyers.com, December 12, 2016, retrieved August 20, 2018.
42. Rebecca M. Taylor, "Taking Seriously Campus Debates Surrounding Invited Speakers: Open-Mindedness and the Ethics of Inquiry in Higher Education," *Teachers College Record* 126(3): 86–109.
43. "Broken Inquiry on Campus," March 12, 2017, https://brokeninquiryblog.wordpress.com. As cited in Rebecca M. Taylor, "Taking Seriously Campus Debates Surrounding Invited Speakers: Open-Mindedness and the Ethics of Inquiry in Higher Education," *Teachers College Record* 126(3): 86–109.
44. John Palfrey, *Safe Spaces, Brave Spaces: Diversity and Free Expression in Education* (Cambridge, MA: MIT Press, 2017), 106.
45. See Louis Michael Seidman, "Can Free Speech Be Progressive?" Georgetown University Law Center, https://scholarship.law.georgetown.edu/facpub/2018, 1–31. accessed May 5, 2019.
46. Jessica Bennett, "What If Instead of Calling People Out, We Called Them In?" *New York Times*, November 19, 2020, D1 and D4.

Works Cited

Ablow, Galil. December 12, 2016. "Talking Back to Hate Speech, Explained." https://billmoyers.com/story/talking-back-hate-speech-explained/. Accessed August 20, 2018.

ACLU. "Free Speech on Campus." https://www.aclu.org. Accessed August 15, 2018.

Baehr, Jason. 2011. *The Inquiring Mind*. Oxford: Oxford University Press.

Ben-Porath, Sigal R. 2017. *Free Speech on Campus*. Philadelphia: University of Pennsylvania Press.

Bennett, Jessica. November 19, 2020. "What If Instead of Calling People Out, We Called Them In?" *New York Times*, D1 and D4.

Bleich, Erik. 2011. "The Rise of Hate Speech and Hate Crime Laws in Liberal Democracies." *Journal of Ethnic and Migration Studies* 37(6): 917–934.

"Broken Inquiry on Campus." March 12, 2017. https://brokeninquiryblog.wordpress.com. As cited in Rebecca M. Taylor, "Taking Seriously Campus Debates Surrounding Invited Peakers: Open-Mindedness and the Ethics of Inquiry in Higher Education." *Teachers College Record* 126(3): 86–109.

Chemerinsky, Erwin and Howard Gillman. 2017. *Free Speech on Campus*. New Haven, CT: Yale University Press.

Criminal Code of Canada, Section 319(2).

Dearden, R. F. 1981. "Controversial Issues in the Curriculum." *Journal of Curriculum Studies* 13: 37–44.

Delgado, Richard and Jean Stefancic. 1997. *Must We Defend Nazis? Hate Speech, Pornography and the New First Amendment.* New York: New York University Press.

Frayn, Michael. 1966. *The Tin Men.* London: Fontana Paperbacks.

Glanville, Doug. May 19, 2019. "Was I Racially Taunted?" *New York Times, Sunday Review,* 2.

Hand, Michael. 2008. "What Should We Teach as Controversial? A Defense of the Epistemic Criterion." *Educational Theory* 58: 213–228.

Hare, William. 1979. *Open-mindedness and Education.* Montreal: McGill-Queen's University Press.

Hare, William. 1985. *In Defense of Open-mindedness.* Montreal: McGill-Queen's University Press.

Heller, Nathan. 2016. "The Big Uneasy: What's Roiling the Liberal Arts Campus?" *New Yorker* 92(16). https://www.newyorker.com/magazine/2016/05/30/the-new-activism-of-liberal-arts-colleges. Accessed August 6, 2018.

Hess, Diana E. and Paula McAvoy. 2015. *The Political Classroom: Evidence and Ethics in the Democratic Classroom.* New York: Routledge.

Hickman, Leo. May 17, 2011. "US School Board Teaches 'the Controversy' on Global Warming." *The Guardian.* https://www.theguardian.com/environment/blog/2011/may/17/global-warming-school-teaching-controversy. Accessed March 15, 2019.

Kutner, Max. March 25, 2016. "Emory Students Explain Why 'Trump 2016' Chalk Messages Triggered Protest." *Newsweek.* https://www.newsweek.com/emory-trump-chalk-protests-440618. Accessed March 17, 2019.

Lambie, John. 2014. *How to Be Critically Open-Minded: A Psychological and Historical Analysis.* Cambridge: Palgrave Macmillan.

Lukianoff, Greg and Jonathan Haidt. September 2015. "The Coddling of the American Mind." *The Atlantic.* https://www.theatlantic.com/magazine/archive/2015/09/the-coddling-of-the-american-mind/399356/. Accessed September 11, 2018.

Moody-Adams, Michele. 2018. "Is There a 'Safe Space' for Academic Freedom?" In *Academic Freedom*, ed. Jennifer Lackey (pp. 36–61). Oxford: Oxford University Press.

Palfrey, John. 2017. *Safe Spaces, Brave Spaces: Diversity and Free Expression in Education.* Cambridge, MA: MIT Press.

Police Dept. of Chicago v. Mosley, 408 U.S. 92 1972.

Riggs, Wayne. 2016. "Open-Mindedness, Insight, and Understanding." In *Intellectual Virtues and Education: Essays in Applied Virtue Epistemology,* ed. Jason Baehr (pp. 18–37). New York: Routledge.

Routledge, Clay. October 14, 2017. "Millennials Are Wary of Freedom." *New York Times, Sunday Review.* https://www.nytimes.com/2017/10/14/opinion/sunday/millennials-freedom-fear.html. Accessed September 12, 2018.

Scott, Eugenie C. 2007. "What's Wrong with the 'Teach the Controversy' Slogan?" *McGill Journal of Education* 42(2): 307–315.

Seidman, Louis Michael. 2019. "Can Free Speech Be Progressive?" Georgetown University Law Center, https://scholarship.law.georgetown.edu/facpub/2018, 1–31. Accessed May 5, 2019.

Song, Yujia. 2017. "The Moral Virtue of Open-Mindedness." *Canadian Journal of Philosophy* 48(1): 1–20.

Taylor, Rebecca. 2024. "Taking Seriously Campus Debates Surrounding Invited Speakers: Open-Mindedness and the Ethics of Inquiry in Higher Education." *Teachers College Record* 126(3): 86–109.

Verducci, Susan. 2019. "The Arts and Open-Mindedness." *Educational Theory* 69(4): 495–401.

Waldron, Jeremy. 2012. *The Harm in Hate Speech*. Cambridge, MA: Harvard University Press.

Warnick, Bryan R. and D. Spencer Smith. 2014. "The Controversy over Controversies: A Plea for Flexibility and for 'Soft-Directive' Teaching." *Educational Theory* 64(3): 227–244.

Warnock, Geoffrey. 1975. "Education and Pluralism: What Sort of Problems?" *Oxford Review of Education* 1(2): 93–97.

Wikipedia. "Milo Yiannopoulos." https://en.wikipedia.org/wiki/Milo_Yiannopoulos. Accessed September 12, 2018.

Yong, Caleb. 2011. "Does Freedom of Speech Include Hate Speech?" *Res Publica* 17: 385–403.

Zimmerman, Jon and Emily Robertson. 2017. *The Case for Contention: Teaching Controversial Issues in American Schools.* Chicago: University of Chicago Press.

5

Jacques Copeau's Theater and Masks: Actor Training as Formation in Open-Mindedness

Margaret (Peggy) Garvey

1 Introduction

The French theater director Jacques Copeau (1879–1949) is the founder of the physical theater movement of the early 1900s. He was once world famous for having radically transformed the art of acting and enhanced its beauty. His physical theater education methods freed his actors from techniques of rote impersonation by training them to engage their full bodies in "incarnating" the fictive character. In order to do this, he employed the now mainstream training methods of improvisation, theater games, and the mask. In this chapter, I show that Copeau formed his actors in open-mindedness—considered by some virtue epistemologists to be a species of epistemic humility—and that this played a crucial role in his success. According to Copeau's understanding, an inherent part of open-mindedness was personal authenticity. His actors sought to express a compelling and audience-inspiring "sincerity" onstage, but this "sincerity" depended on "real-life" authenticity or simplicity in the actor as a human being. This dependency makes Copeau's use of masks paradoxical: to capacitate actors in the art of donning the mask of fictional characters, of completely identifying with each one, he educated them in the ability to remove the inner, invisible mask of social persona. In this way, they could mitigate any tendency toward pretension in interpersonal

Margaret (Peggy) Garvey, *Jacques Copeau's Theater and Masks: Actor Training as Formation in Open-Mindedness* In: *The Virtue of Open-Mindedness and Perspective*. Edited by: Wayne D. Riggs, Oxford University Press. © Oxford University Press 2025. DOI: 10.1093/9780190080723.003.0006

JACQUES COPEAU'S THEATER AND MASKS   123

relationships in their lives offstage and, consequently, in their melding with the fictional character onstage.

This description of Copeau's methods might be baffling to those new to theater studies or whose common sense leads them to balk at the idea that training for the art of "putting on an act" is connected to any version of the virtues of sincerity, simplicity, or open-mindedness. Theater academics and experts almost certainly will find my characterization of Copeau's methods to be novel and controversial. They are. This is because among theater scholars and practitioners Copeau's emphasis on the physicality of acting and his use of masks is considered a consequence of a Nietzschean modernism. Nietzsche glorified the mask only as an analogy for the opaque nature of human action, never as a means for growing in authenticity; his radical perspectivalism deliberately encouraged turning one's back on a reality not purely of one's own subjective creation—the exact opposite of open-mindedness or epistemic humility.

I argue that Copeau's pedagogy and its promotion of growth in open-mindedness is due to the influence of an Aristotelian thinker of the time—Maria Montessori (1870–1952). Her influence on Copeau and his emphasis on the actor's practice of authenticity has only recently been uncovered and until now has been left unexamined. The consequences of this controversial shifting of the philosophical tradition to which Copeau belongs from Nietzsche to Aristotle are not insignificant for either the layperson's or the scholar's understanding of the virtue of open-mindedness and the way to acquire it.

Montessori's work in educational philosophy and psychology played a fundamental role in shaping Copeau's approach to the actor and the art of theater. Copeau's drama school, Le Vieux Colombier[1] (which was the progenitor of Juilliard and the Royal Academy of Dramatic Acting, among other schools), was inspired by Montessori's then-radical principles of education and developmental psychology. Her ideas inspired both Copeau's theater and performance curriculum and his philosophy as theater director. Most important, he and his key assistant, the actress Suzanne Bing, based their actor education on Montessori's learning principles of childlike wonder, keen observation, and the exercise of free, physically adept, interest-driven movement and play. Bing transcribed eleven pages of the first edition of the

124 THE VIRTUE OF OPEN-MINDEDNESS

Montessori Method[2] and trained for a few months at a Montessori school while the troupe was in the United States. She then worked with Copeau to invent methods of actor training built on Montessori's methods: games, animal imitation exercises, and techniques of improvisation based on stories. Copeau fully embraced Montessori's belief that imitating the child's capacity for wonder and simplicity was a path toward the intellectual rigor and the virtues of a true scientist as well as a path to the joy and freedom that invigorate all work and increase personal authenticity.

In Copeau's archives lies the trajectory of his child-centered research into masks.[3] His sketches and notes show how he reflected on the effect that masks of different types had on children and their capacity to overcome fear and practice sincerity. His integration of masks into acting pedagogy was a stunningly unique application of his Montessorian beliefs. In combination, Copeau's use of masks and his philosophy of theater provide a surprising but indisputable witness to the central role of the virtue of open-mindedness in the theater actor's art. They also testify to the fact that Copeau's body-centered, physical acting was founded on a philosophy of the person and of virtue based on Montessori and the Aristotelian tradition.[4]

Theater scholars have long wrestled with the conundrum presented by Copeau—a true "modernist" and acknowledged inspiration behind the most "physical" contemporary acting methods and theater traditions including mime, improvisation, and theater games.[5] Masks and a body-centered aesthetic (as opposed to an aesthetic of "the word"—a more literary theater) are associated with modernism's icon, Friedrich Nietzsche. My claim states that although his methods are centered on body and instinct, Copeau subverts Nietzschean tenets in multiple ways—by insisting on the integration of instincts and physicality with intellect and virtue; by masking the actor not to allow her to hide, but to force her to reveal herself; by despising acting emanating from a worldview tinged by a disregard for outside reality, the truth outside of oneself. Nietzsche's radically subjective perspectivalism could have no part in the virtue of open-mindedness or epistemic humility Copeau insisted on for his actors.

The reason for the seeming conundrum and ensuing mystification is that Copeau's connection with Montessori has been

JACQUES COPEAU'S THEATER AND MASKS   125

mostly overlooked, and where it has been noted, the philosophical consequences have been deemed inconsequential.[6] Montessori's child-centered principles and Thomist-Aristotelian epistemology and psychology shaped Copeau's worldview and guided him at every turn in his journey toward optimal actor training. Copeau's "physical theater" was a theater that inculcated the learning child's simplicity and wonder in its performers. It could more accurately be called a theater of embodied, Montessorian learning. Contemporary epistemology would describe this as a theater-making dependent on an especially robust open-mindedness and driven by Montessori's unique version of epistemic love. For Montessori, this is the love contained in "wonder" and defined as the intellectual desire to come to know an already beloved reality, not simply a desire for the attainment of knowledge for itself.

2 Copeau's Montessorian Theater: Authenticity, Freedom for Intentional Movement and Love for the World Outside of Oneself

For Copeau, epistemic love was the capacity to wonder at and pay full attention to outside reality. Copeau was convinced that good theater was born of authentic actors, free interiorly to practice open-mindedness—to absorb the outside world and the full reality of others, including their own fictive characters. Copeau instilled in his actors the motivation of epistemic love—the capacity to wonder—to inspire this openness.

Copeau worried that the "cabotin" or actor of his day was disconnected from "outside reality."[7] Disgusted with ham acting on the stage in Paris, Copeau accused these actors all of a lack of intelligence, of simplicity,[8] and of a sense of the morality of their art.[9] He perceived in the young adult actors he worked with a few years later a narcissism that led them to think "only about themselves," "to love only themselves." Because of this, the actors' imaginations were dulled; they resorted to tricks of the trade since they did not possess the resources for creating unique, living renditions of the characters they sought to portray.

126   THE VIRTUE OF OPEN-MINDEDNESS

By contrast, in his own research Copeau followed Montessori's methodology of childlike observation.[10] He keenly contemplated his own children and the children who joined his experimental lab theater school (first begun in seedling form in 1913 and solidified in 1921),[11] and this led him to believe, like Montessori, that interested and intentional, physically adept, freely chosen movement was crucial for the actor's spirit, intellect, and creativity. It made acting joyful and compelling, and drew audiences into the action onstage, eliciting involuntary and pleasurable attention.[12] With an intellect and imagination vivified by interest and freed exteriorly and interiorly to express itself through the body, the actor could incarnate a character rather than merely imitate its superficial behaviors.

Two arenas contained obstacles for freely chosen, love- or wonder-inspired movement. The first was the cluttered stage. Employing a Montessorian procedure[13] Copeau made the bare stage a trademark of his productions. The second was the actor's hampered interiority. This posed a much more difficult problem. Copeau developed a highly disciplined yet spontaneous version of the now mainstream practice of "improve"[14] but realized that interior freedom was not guaranteed by its use alone. Interior freedom was linked to the ability to act spontaneously on the basis of personal initiative and interest in the outside world; it was also mysteriously linked to authenticity, simplicity, and sincerity—terms Copeau used interchangeably. He considered these three words to be synonyms for denoting both an important characteristic of the actor as a human person and the hallmarks of excellent acting. Simplicity was a virtue that Copeau associated with happy, playful children. "Sincere" acting seamlessly integrated emotion and physical action.[15] It often indicated absolute concentration, the state of psychological "flow"[16] or full immersion in action onstage. Thus Copeau defined play for the actor just as Montessori did for her children. It was "work-play" or free movement inspired by interest born of "psychic instincts"[17] in a carefully organized "prepared environment." "Work-play" and a potential state of "flow" come about within an intellectually stimulating—a "[learning]-prepared"—environment replete with physical objects that develop and refine the senses.[18] Copeau's version of the Montessorian prepared learning environment[19] was the integration of training in sculpting and crafts and his

JACQUES COPEAU'S THEATER AND MASKS   127

use of improvisation scenarios from Commedia dell' Arte (involving broad but clearly delineated roles and plots). Full immersion in and physical interaction with the world around them nourished the young actors' free and innate intellectual desire. It was obvious to Copeau that this educational atmosphere increased joy, facilitated the state of "flow," intensified concentration and enhanced deep, personalized absorption of outside reality.

For Copeau, the capacity for childlike "work-play"[20] was the guarantee of onstage acting that was free and spontaneous—"sincere." The idea that theatrical "sincerity" could be dependent on the psychological foundations of play which is, in turn, conducive to a highly self-disciplining style of learning, is counterintuitive. But Copeau's research with child-actors convinced him of this beyond any doubt, so much so that he called the actor's identification with a fictive character as a spontaneity that was "sought" or a "worked sincerity."[21] Onstage sincerity/simplicity is the unobstructed identification of the authentic self of the actor with the character being portrayed; offstage, it is equivalent to the actor's interior unification of action and intention and its transparent expression, her personal authenticity.

Copeau stressed that this personal authenticity was a sine qua non for work-play itself because for him it represented more than an acquired virtue. It was a state of mind and emotion; a state of peace and self-awareness without self-consciousness and within an environment of learning and interacting with one's physical surroundings and companions. Not only play and learning, but also the ability to incarnate a character sprang from the ability to reach and act from within this primal state.[22] In this he appropriated the concept of "normalization"[23] from Montessori—a prerequisite emotional and psychological modus operandi for her children. For Montessori and Copeau it was necessary to be in a state of peaceful, interiorly recollected, happy self-awareness—a "normalized" state—to be capable of self-possessed movement and concentrated work.

Copeau developed an authoritative yet kind relationship with his actors to achieve this normalization or "state of simplicity" that invited and was equated with authenticity. In doing so, he demonstrated that this state depended on the awareness of being loved that builds self-confidence and promotes the fearless embracing of one's own

128   THE VIRTUE OF OPEN-MINDEDNESS

vulnerability.[24] Copeau's archival notes indicate that he sensed a lack of simplicity or transparency in action to be an unhealthy "mask on the heart,"[25] precluding openness to the outside world, deep relationships, and seamless stage acting. This mask "on the heart" is the Nietzschean mask mentioned in the introduction, the mask that hides the authentic self and thus becomes an obstacle to personal authenticity.

The childlike "state of simplicity," or embodied mindfulness[26] and foundation for authenticity, was, according to Copeau, basic to the expansion of a distinct kind of imaginative power. Copeau perceived that contact and interaction with physical reality developed the imagination and intellect simultaneously. The vividness and resilience of the imagination depended on the mind's ability to draw accurate perceptions from reality constantly.[27] Copeau rejected reality-detached, false creativity. Montessori emphatically condemned an education that trained the imagination to indulge in "flights into fantasy" or was triggered by fear.[28] Educators who substituted their own imaginative construct for the fruit of their students' creative work[29] were dulling their students' minds and imaginations. Copeau, was similarly ruthless in denouncing acting fed on "illusions" and superficial appropriations of gestures, makeup, or props.[30] His neutral mask training and Montessorian education of the imagination ensured that the actor could identify with any character (sometimes crystallized in a character mask) at the deepest level and produce in-character, yet spontaneous and consistently fresh gestures.

3   Copeau's Masks

To enrich his actors' imaginations and instill open-mindedness, Copeau was determined to increase his actors' access to two kinds of simplicity—the "state" (which was the basis for all personal authenticity and authentic action on- and offstage) and the "practice" (the enactment of a fully blown fictive character without interpolation from the actor's own personality). This determination gave rise to the most fascinating innovation—and the most putatively "Nietzschean" element as mentioned above—in Copeau's actor training: the use of masks.

JACQUES COPEAU'S THEATER AND MASKS   129

David Wiles, the most recent and influential theater scholar to cast Copeau as a Nietzschean, never even considers that Copeau might have culled his philosophical anthropology and epistemology from Aristotle via Montessori instead. In his study of the history of the mask and its use, he concludes that history must accept Copeau as the conundrum mentioned above, that he is simply an unusual Nietzschean.[31] Yet Copeau's understanding of the mask is diametrically opposed to Nietzsche's. Nietzsche saw the mask as symbolic of the human being's need to become a different person in each relationship, a symbol of the opaque nature of action,[32] and the exteriorization and hardening of the "mask on the heart" that Copeau, as we saw above, cited as a major obstacle to personal authenticity. Copeau, in stark contrast, saw the use of masks as an opportunity to grow in transparency in action—in simplicity first as a state, then, as a practice.

Copeau first experimented with the "noble" or "neutral"—expressionless—mask starting in 1921, the very beginning of his more established theater school.[33] Later, he began using the "character" mask[34] as part of actor training and productions of a "new commedia"[35] original works arising from fictional plots and characters often invented by the actors themselves.

Intrigued by evidence indicating that children could express themselves more freely and sincerely when masked, he began experiments with the "noble" or neutral mask with the young students in his school among whom were his daughter, Marie-Elene or Maiene, and his future son-in-law, Jean Dasté.[36]

At Copeau's insistence, the young actors themselves made the masks (with the help of a sculptor) to resemble their own faces in a neutral expression.[37] He and Suzanne Bing developed rituals and exercises utilizing the neutral mask. These included respectfully handling and quietly contemplating the mask as one sat and collected all one's powers of concentration, striving to achieve the "state of childlike simplicity."[38] After a time, the actor would put the mask on and slowly move around the space. Eventually the actors began to use these masks in group improvisations, moving from simple to more complex scenarios.[39] The student actors' reactions were remarkable: "They at once reported a new sense of confidence and authority, "a power and

130   THE VIRTUE OF OPEN-MINDEDNESS

unknown security—a sort of balance and consciousness of each gesture and of oneself."[40]

The "mask on the heart"—the self-consciousness and artificiality—which obstructed the actor's authentic personality was dissolved and the embodied experience of a state of simplicity and mind-body unity led to greater transparency of action-intention. The actors, like Montessorian child-learners, were freer to follow "psychic instincts" and the innate instinct of wonder, since the mask ironically forced them to shed the "mask of the heart" or social persona, embrace their vulnerability, and trust in their environment.

Copeau's innovative research with the neutral mask led him to experiment with "character masks"—not unlike those of Greek tragedy or Commedia dell' Arte in which a character is epitomized in a fixed expression. The actors again made these masks themselves while simultaneously inventing the mask's character/personality. They approached them by means of the same ritual as the neutral mask—the focused contemplative gaze in stillness—following this with the embodying of the character through slow movement and improvisation.[41]

Copeau spoke of these character masks as objects that catalyzed and crystallized the process of an actor representing a *dramatis persona*. In his manifesto on acting, *Réflexions sur le Paradox de Diderot*,[42] Copeau explains that a truly versatile actor—one who imitates the learning child—can literally allow a character to take complete ownership of her body and mind, her imagination, emotions and intellect, and never lose her sense of self. She can don the character mask physically or imaginatively, and allow its "persona" to take possession of her without compromising her own personal integrity.[43] Hence, the well-trained actor can summon up the concentration, mindfulness, and body-mind integration that the neutral mask facilitates, maintaining that sense of self while imaginatively identifying with the character and allowing her body to creatively manifest all of the character's bodily traits and expressions.

Copeau's manifesto uses passive language to describe the actor's interaction with the character who "inhabits" her and "comes to" her. His words reflect the fact that, trained in childlike wonder, Copeau's actor creates the character by means of a vivid imagination nourished by intelligent, sense-based exploration of the real. Creating the character mask with her own hands, she inscribes characteristic features in the mask's facial expression. Her whole embodied intellect can then identify with the fictive character's mask and enter a state of mutual "possession" [the actor possessing the character by means of in-depth, sense-based intellectual knowledge of her imagined character and the character mask "possessing" the actor's intellect and imagination by means of fully engaging her attention and expressing itself through the body of the actor]. The learning child, too, in a state of psychological flow, becomes one with the object with which she is interacting and is fully immersed in her actions.

Copeau does not shy away from the danger of "losing" oneself in portrayals of fictive characters. He confidently affirms, however, that this is overcome by the actor's "possessing" herself first through child-like simplicity or personal authenticity—that state of mind and virtue taught by means of the exercises with the neutral mask. This strong personal authenticity combined with the character mask training rituals taught the actor simultaneously "to identify with and distinguish herself from" the character while on stage.[44]

4 Contemporary Virtue Epistemology and the Montessorian Copeau

Copeau's actor-education methods were fundamentally a process of virtue-formation—specifically, the virtues of epistemic love and epistemic humility. What we now call open-mindedness is in Montessori's epistemology an aspect of the latter.

The contemporary virtue epistemologist Jason Baehr defines open-mindedness as "a kind of cognitive detaching from or transcending of a default cognitive standpoint."[45] It is the ability to resist the urge to make the world conform to one's own ideas.[46] Epistemic humility in this school of thought is similar but is conceived of as a specifically social virtue involving deference toward the perspectives of others, a virtue that contrasts essentially with the vice of vanity.

By contrast, Copeau's actor-training methods aimed to foster the more Montessorian combination of these virtues—"the cognitive detaching" in the face of reality and "epistemic humility" in

132   THE VIRTUE OF OPEN-MINDEDNESS

interpersonal relations. That is, Copeau's is an epistemic humility that involved first, deference toward the objectively real world, and second, the interpersonal expression of respect for the perspectives of others. As Patrick Frierson, the sole contemporary philosopher who has analyzed Montessori's epistemology, points out, Montessorian epistemic humility identifies more closely with the open-mindedness of contemporary virtue epistemology and yet contains within it the contemporary version of epistemic humility as well:

> But, for her, this epistemic arrogance is not primarily interpersonal but is, rather, an insistence that the world conform to one's ideas. This conception of intellectual humility is closer to "open-mindedness" [Zagzebski 1996: 114; Baehr 2011b] or, better, the "firmness'" that Roberts and Wood oppose to the vice of "rigidity" [2007: 184, 193f.]. But the concept of "humility" rightly captures the common element shared between a willingness to subject oneself to what is given by nature, to humble oneself before the tasks required by the pursuit of knowledge, and to approach other people with unassuming openness to their points of view.

Frierson in the article cited highlights that Montessori's epistemology has unique and illuminating facets capable of contributing to current virtue epistemology. Epistemic humility for her, as for Copeau, was humility before a world *which one loves*, a resistance to imposing one's own cherished views or theories on the world or on any human being because of this love:

> As Montessori's scientist shows, while humility is first and foremost humility before the *world that one loves*, it also requires humility before other people. The scientist "assume[s] the position of one who is seeking the truth together with his pupils, and invit[es] them to verify it" (Montessori, Spontaneous Activity in Education, 105) Humility before nature and before other human beings go hand in hand, and the true *virtues* of humility-before-nature and humility-before-others mutually reinforce one another. For all of the reasons that intellectual humility is valuable in humans' corporate search for knowledge (see Roberts and Wood [2007: 250–255]), one who is truly humble before nature will be humble before others.[47]

JACQUES COPEAU'S THEATER AND MASKS 133

Humility-before-nature and humility-before-others are Copeau's version of open-mindedness that in turn is intensified by epistemic love. Copeau fomented intellectual love in his actors just as Montessori did in her students. This version of intellectual love is the capacity to wonder at reality and not merely to love knowledge per se. Copeau engaged them in activities that honed their concentration, observation, and attention skills. He trained them in skilled physical dexterity and helped them envision their craft as involvement in something greater than themselves. They thus gained a sense of the beauty of their art as a mission, a vocation to serve an objective reality beyond themselves—the poet's text, the ensemble, and the audience for whom they performed.

Shaping and manipulating the neutral masks of their own faces, the actors gazed on their own mind-body unity, their intimate inner selves stripped of any "mask on the heart." Following that, they created the personality and outward features of their character mask. This second mask-making engaged all their powers of wonder and attention, reinforced by the inner freedom of authenticity gained by the use of the neutral mask. Hence, they could more fully focus on another "self," the fruit of their own imagination shaped by attentive observation of reality. The union or "marriage" of these neutral and character mask exercises empowered them for the child-learner's freedom and joy that Copeau insisted was inherent to being a successful actor.

In Copeau's theater, authenticity decluttered the actor's inner world. Vanity could no longer get in the way of showing epistemic humility toward other people. Simultaneously, and more important for Copeau, "wonder" brought with it "open-mindedness"—a child-learner's desire to humble herself before a beloved reality. Both Copeau's neutral mask and character mask use are manifestations of the power of authenticity to nourish love for reality and open-mindedness. Copeau's neutral and character masks crystallized the two types of authenticity required for the actor's craft—personal simplicity and sincerity in characterization. They also clarify the connection between growth in personal authenticity, the capacity for wonder, and the sincere incarnation of a fictive character.

Open-mindedness for Copeau then is paradigmatically a virtue of the humble, open-hearted, learning child. It has to be born of love and sustained by it. It cannot be just detachment from a cognitive standpoint or politeness—a deferential "openness" to another's opinion or

134   THE VIRTUE OF OPEN-MINDEDNESS

worldview.[48] Epistemic humility is a requirement for learning, and epistemic love for the reality that one is intellectually absorbing is the motor for continued and more in-depth learning. The marriage of Copeau's neutral and character masks in the acting process symbolizes a path toward the practice of an especially strong open-mindedness. The contemplation of her unified "self" in the neutral mask both strips an individual of inauthentic, vain, self-conscious preoccupations and prepares her to wonder at, love, and be more active in learning about the outside world. In Copeau's theatrical world, intellectual love and intellectual humility invigorate and ground one another. The actor's craft demands an open-mindedness that is intrigued by the perspectives of others, since, they, like all of reality, inspire genuine awe.

Notes

1. A modified version of this educational philosophy became the basis of the curricula of the most renowned contemporary acting schools (Juilliard in New York, Royal Academy of Dramatic Art (RADA) in London, and the École Internationale de Théâtre of Jacques Lecoq, to mention only a few). Unfortunately, Copeau's nephew Michel Saint-Denis, who helped found Juilliard and RADA, never fully grasped the reasons for the centrality of Montessorian observation of the learning child for insights into personal authenticity and truly creative acting or the significance of Copeau's notion of "sincerity" for the actor and her process. (Cf chapter 5, "Jacques Copeau, Maria Montessori and a Physical Theatre of Aristotelian Embodiment," dissertation by Margaret Garvey, University of Notre Dame, 2014.)
2. Maria Montessori, Notes de travail; Ms. de Suzanne Bing, Dossier 2/3 l'École du Vieux Colombier, Fonds Copeau, Bibliothèque nationale de France, Paris. The words handwritten, studied, and absorbed by Bing from *The Montessori Method. Scientific Pedagogy as Applied to Child Education in the "Children's Houses" with Additions and Revisions by the Author.* trans. Ann E. George (New York: Frederick A. Stokes, 1912), 6–11, show concrete evidence of the source of Copeau's thinking on the observation of children, much of which is compiled in Jacques Copeau, *Copeau: Texts on Theater*, ed. John Rudlin and Norman Paul (London: Routledge, 1990) (cf. my analysis in Garvey, dissertation, 34–37).
3. Jacques Copeau, "ORCH MASQUE CROQUIS ET NOTES" COTE – 4-COL 1/ 291 (39–4), Fonds Copeau, Bibliothèque nationale de France Paris.
4. In my dissertation, I argue that Montessori and Copeau were Aristotelians in their educational philosophy. Kristjan Kristjansson describes this tradition of educational philosophy as built on four "fusions": the fusion of action and emotion; the fusion of the biological, moral, and political natures of the human being; the fusion of theory and practice; and the fusion of self and others. Kristjansson, *Aristotle, Emotions, and Education* (Aldershot, England: Ashgate, 2007), 176–177. E. M. Standing in *The Child in the Church* (St. Paul, Minnesota: Catechetical Guide, 1965) analyzes Montessori's work within a scholastic framework (i.e., within the philosophical tradition of Aristotelianism mediated through the medieval philosopher Thomas Aquinas). But Standing's analysis is brief and in my view somewhat

JACQUES COPEAU'S THEATER AND MASKS 135

misleading. The more recent analysis in David T. Hansen, ed. *Ethical Visions of Education, Philosophies in Practice* (New York: Teachers' College Press, Columbia University, 2007), 111–125, develops the ethical notions inherent in her philosophy in the chapter "Peace as a Premise for Learning: Maria Montessori's Educational Philosophy," but refrains from attempting to identify any one philosophical tradition to which they belong or to look at other philosophical dimensions besides the ethical. Although Patrick Frierson, a philosopher who currently works on Montessori, sees a Nietzschean influence on Montessori's virtue epistemology, I hold to the view that when approached synthetically and in the light of a Thomist Aristotelianism and the religious tradition that she took for granted and refers to constantly, Montessori is first and foremost Aristotelian.

5. Among them Mark Evans in *Jacques Copeau*, ed. Franc Chamberlain (London: Routledge, Taylor & Francis Group, 2006); David Wiles in *Mask and Performance in Greek Tragedy: From Ancient Festival to Modern Experimentation* (Cambridge: Cambridge University Press, 2007), and Mark Fortier, in *Theory/ Theatre: An Introduction* (London: Routledge, 2002).

6. Patrick Frierson, to my knowledge the only philosopher currently working on the philosophical analysis of Montessori's theory and practice, presents a succinct account of her virtue epistemology and its unique nature in his article "The Virtue Epistemology of Maria Montessori," *Australasian Journal of Philosophy* 94(1) (2016): 79–98. And for a longer version of her virtue epistemology, cf. *Intellectual Agency and Virtue Epistemology: A Montessori Perspective* (New York: Bloomsbury Academic, 2021).

7. From Michel Saint-Denis, *Training for the Theatre* (New York: Theatre Arts; London: Heinemann), 31, quoted in John Rudlin, "Jacques Copeau, the Quest for Sincerity," in *Twentieth Century Actor Training*, ed. Alison Hodge (pp. 55–78) (London: Routledge, 2000).

8. Copeau's diaries and writings are rife with criticism of society in general, actors and individuals whom he assessed as lacking simplicity. On actors in just one instance, see *Copeau, Registres I: Appels, Notes by Claude Sicard* (Paris: Gallimard, 1974), 123.

9. *Copeau, Registres I: Appels, Notes by Claude Sicard* (Paris: Gallimard, 1974), 28.

10. Cf. *Copeau, Registres IV-Les Registres du Vieux Colombier II. American Notes by N. Paul*, ed. Marie Hélène Dasté and Suzanne Maistre Saint-Denis (Paris: Gallimard, 1984), 512–513.

11. The history of his school and theater are thoroughly researched by Barbara Leigh Kusler in her unpublished dissertation "Jacques Copeau's Theatre School: L'Ecole du Vieux Colombie, 1920–1929," University of Wisconsin, 1974.

12. Copeau insisted that acting "is the last of all crafts if it is made up of grimaces, servility, if it is not sincere and joyful." *Registres IV-Les Registres Du Vieux Colombier II. American Notes by N. Paul*, 503. He also spoke of the play of happy children as "rejuvenating" and compelling the involvement of the adults watching them. Copeau, *Copeau: Texts on Theatre*, ed. John Rudlin and Norman Paul (London: Routledge, 1990), 9.

13. For an analysis of how Adolphe Appia and Copeau mutually influenced one another, in particular Copeau's transformative effect on Appia's ideas of the musical foundations of theater and its architecture, see Garvey dissertation, 194–202. By means of their exchange of ideas from 1916 to 1922, Appia began to fully embrace Copeau's primacy of the actor and the "music of stage action" and the music of stage architecture as subordinate in its function. Also see Copeau, *Copeau: Texts on Theater*, ed. John Rudlin and Norman Paul, 93–101.

14. Copeau became such an expert Montessorian innovator that he even convinced the founder of the school that Bing attended—Margaret Frank, herself trained by Montessori—of the importance of incorporating improv of this type into her

136 THE VIRTUE OF OPEN-MINDEDNESS

curriculum. Jacques Copeau, *Registres IV-Les Registres Du Vieux Colombier II. American Notes by N. Paul* (Paris: Gallimard, 1984), 514.

15. Rudlin's article, "Jacques Copeau. The Quest for Sincerity," 63–66, quotes Copeau as referring to this foundational sincerity as a "naïve state" and explains it as "discovering dramatic principles within oneself, embracing the naïve without intellectual reservation, developing an authenticity of gesture to emotional impulse."

16. Though not the main topic of this chapter, Copeau's psychology also overlaps in significant ways with the psychology of flow of Mihaly Csikszentmihalyi, cf. *Flow, the Psychology of Optimal Experience* (New York: Harper Perennial, 1991). Copeau's description of the immersion in stage action that he wished his actors to achieve is redolent of descriptions of persons in psychological "flow." Cf. the description of his son-in-law in Copeau, *Copeau: Texts on Theater*, ed. John Rudlin and Norman Paul, 238. from *Qui êtes-vous?* (Lyons: La Manufacture, 1987) and Rudlin's equation of Copeau's pinnacle of acting with the state of flow in Rudlin, "Play's the Thing," *Mime Journal, 1996,* 26–27. Rudlin here does not include Montessori in his review of psychologists who have noted the significance of play in education.

17. A Montessorian term indicating that children will, if left to these psychic instincts, choose "intelligent objects" and spontaneously want to work with their developing intellects. Montessori, *Spontaneous Activity in Education* (New York: Schocken Books, 1965), 195.

18. Montessori, *Spontaneous Activity in Education*, 195.

19. *Copeau: Texts on Theater*, ed. John Rudlin and Norman Paul, 49, and Garvey dissertation, 77.

20. Montessorian work-play can be productive, serious work, but it foregrounds free personal choice, interest, full intellectual and emotional engagement in action, and an attitude of enjoyment.

21. Copeau, *Registres I: Appels, Notes by Claude Sicard*, 207.

22. Rudlin, *Jacques Copeau*, Directors in Perspective, edited by Christopher Innes (Cambridge: Cambridge University Press, 1986), 46, quoting Copeau's diary of 1919: "The point of departure of an expression. The state of repose, of calm, of relaxation or decontraction, of silence or simplicity . . . premeditated, . . . felt."

23. Patrick Frierson, *The Moral Philosophy of Maria Montessori: Agency and Ethical Life* (London: Bloomsbury Academic, 2022), 220, note 8, defines normalization as a "technical term" that "refers to the condition of a child left in freedom in an environment conducive to independent activity, that is, a child who has not been subject to neglect or oppressions that cause psychological deviations." Foucault used this term in the exact opposite sense of Montessori.

24. Copeau on the relationship he strove to have with each of his actors Copeau, *Registres IV-Les Registres Du Vieux Colombier II; American Notes by N. Paul*, 509.

25. Jacques Copeau, "ORCH MASQUE CROQUIS ET NOTES " COTE – 4-COL 1/ 291 (39-4), Fonds Copeau, Bibliothèque nationale de France, Paris. Cf. Garvey dissertation, 116.

26. Darcia Narvaez, the developmental psychologist, defines mindfulness thus: "attending to the embodied experience in the here and now. It means being physically, emotionally, and cognitively present to what is happening in oneself and the vicinity. Learning to live in the present moment is not so much a matter of stillness as it is a way to practice beingness. . . . A mindful attitude lets the emotions come and go, not feeding any one in particular." Darcia Narvaez, *Neurobiology and the Development of Human Morality: Evolution, Culture, Wisdom* (New York: W.W. Norton, 2014), 269.

27. Montessori's description of the artist's powers of imagination as dependent on creativity of a mind "rooted in the observation of reality." Montessori, *Spontaneous Activity in Education*, 250–251.

JACQUES COPEAU'S THEATER AND MASKS 137

28. Montessori, *The Secret of Childhood*, Translated by M. Joseph Costelloe (Notre Dame, IN: Fides Publishers Inc, 1966), 192. Here Montessori stresses that the imagination must be always "firmly allied to reality." Elsewhere in the same book (p. 266), she states, "Imagination un-sustained by truth consumes the intelligence until it assumes characteristics akin to the mental characteristics of the insane." Montessori criticized adults who superficially judged an ungrounded use of the imagination on the part of children as "creativity" asserting that this kind of false creative life would be short-lived and never as rich as an imagination steeped in accurate perceptions from reality itself. Copeau's critique of actors echoed this assessment exactly. Those who approached their fictive characters with "too much ease" and at first glance were highly creative, were in the end the least secure in their performance and the least innovative. *Jacques Copeau, Notes sur le métier du comédien*, ed. Michel Brient (Paris: Michel Brient, 1955), 25.
29. Maria Montessori, *The California Lectures of Maria Montessori, 1915* (Oxford: Cleo, 1997), 43.
30. Copeau, *Registres IV-Les Registres du Vieux Colombier II. American Notes by N. Paul*, 510. Copeau here describes the pitiful case of a young woman who, in striving to become a tragic actress, took medication and put on makeup to increase her pallor and "declaimed" in the manner of the acting of the day.
31. Wiles, *Mask and Performance in Greek Tragedy*, 105. Cf. Garvey dissertation for my critique against Wiles's philosophical analysis of Copeau as Nietzschean, 10, 15, 124.
32. Wiles, *Mask and Performance in Greek Tragedy*, 78. Wiles, here, is quoting from Nietzsche's *The Gay Science*, trans. J. Nauckhoff (Cambridge: Cambridge University Press, 2001) and synthesizing Nietzsche's view of the mask.
33. The noble or neutral mask is an expressionless mask often though not always of the actor's own face. In a fascinating, unpublished archival document, Saint-Denis, Copeau's nephew, and Dasté, his son-in-law, dialogue about when Copeau first began using masks. Dasté insists that they were used from the very start in the lab school, while Saint-Denis was in the theater with older actors. (Saint-Denis in "Dialogue Avec Jean Dasté, 1958", Papers Relating to Jacques Copeau, ADD 81138, Saint Denis Archives, British Library, London, 4–5). Saint-Denis, who brought the curriculum of the Vieux Colombier School to Juilliard and the other contemporary schools mentioned above, did not have firsthand experience of the rituals and hands-on experiential learning associated with the neutral mask. It is not surprising then that in his writings and in what he passed on to these schools was a Vieux Colombier curriculum sans child-centered philosophy and sans emphasis on the child-like state. John Rudlin, "Jacques Copeau. The Quest for Sincerity," 72. Saint-Denis cites a moment in rehearsal when Copeau put a handkerchief on the face of an actress whose "blood had frozen" on stage and the magical influence this had on her ability to shake off her self-consciousness.
34. The character mask, in contrast to the neutral one, is a mask that expresses the essence of a fictive character, similar to the ones used in the theater of ancient Greece. In the same archival document as above, Daste describes a gradual introduction of the character mask in the school after an abundant use of the neutral or "noble" one.
35. The development of this new comedy took place over years of research and dialogue, finally coming to fruition in the first ensemble formed from the school—Les Copiaus. Cf. Rudlin's *Jacques Copeau, Directors in Perspective*, chapter 7.
36. Daste passed on his convictions regarding the importance of this mask to Jacques Lecoq who instituted the use of the more generically neutral mask in his schools. For insights into the differences between Copeau/Daste's use and understanding of the neutral and noble masks and Lecoq's, see Garvey dissertation, 231.

138   THE VIRTUE OF OPEN-MINDEDNESS

37. Michel Saint-Denis, "Dialogue avec Jean Dasté, 1958," Papers Relating to Jacques Copeau, ADD 81138, Saint-Denis Archives, British Library, London.
38. Suzanne Bing, "Cahier Orange, #2" Fonds Copeau, Bibliothèque nationale de France, Paris. Bing describes this state as not "empty" but preformative of action; a state of "recollection" of "simplicity". Through the years, those influenced by Copeau have given it different nomenclature, some veering more toward a Buddhist sense of "emptying" the psyche. In Rudlin, *Jacques Copeau*, Directors in Perspective, 46 quoting Copeau's Notebook of May 1918 and Copeau, *Notes sur le métier du comédien*, ed. Michel Brient (Paris: Michel Brient, 1955), 47, Copeau's vocabulary is the same. Both Copeau and Bing used the vocabulary more resonant of Montessori's sense of a child "at peace" or "normalized" which has a more direct link to a Thomist/Aristotelian understanding of mindfulness and body-soul integration, versus the Eastern, Buddhist ones.
39. Rudlin, *Jacques Copeau*, Directors in Perspective, 48.
40. Rudlin, *Jacques Copeau*, Directors in Perspective, 48, from Marie-Helene Copeau, Notebook 1924 in Barbara Broomall Kusler, "Jacques Copeau's Theater School: L'Ecole du Vieux-Colombier, 1920-1929," Dissertation, University of Wisconsin, Madison, 1974, 117.
41. Thomas Leabhart, "Jacques Copeau, Etienne Decroux and the Flower of Noh," *New Theatre Quarterly* 20(04) (2004): 320.
42. Copeau, Registres I: Appels, Notes by Claude Sicard, 210 from Brient, *Jacques Copeau, Notes sur le métier du comédien*.
43. This "possession" is an embodied, imaginative "identification" with the character, not, as some have argued, a theatrical shamanism. Thomas Leabhart in "Jacques Copeau, Etienne Decroux and the Flower of Noh," argues for a shamanistic interpretation. It is abundantly clear to me, however, that in both Copeau's *Notes sur le métier du comédien* and the texts compiled in Copeau, *Registres I: Appels, Notes by Claude Sicard* that Copeau realized the dangers involved for the actor not sufficiently well trained in authenticity or his "simplicity" (a trait not necessarily demanded of the shaman) as the basis of acting technique, and indeed he points out that the actor risks becoming "denatured" by her craft if not trained on this basis. Copeau, *Registres I: Appels, Notes by Claude Sicard*, 206.
44. Copeau, *Registres I: Appels, Notes by Claude Sicard*, 210.
45. Baehr, Jason, *The Inquiring Mind: On Intellectual Virtues and Virtue Epistemology* (London: Oxford University Press, 2012), 162.
46. Frierson 2016 references Linda Zagzebski in *Virtues of the Mind: An Inquiry into the Nature of Virtue and the Ethical Foundations of Knowledge* (Cambridge: Cambridge University Press, 1996), 114 and Jason Baehr, "The Structure of Open-Mindedness," *Canadian Journal of Philosophy* 41(2) (2011): 191–214.
47. Frierson, 2016, (96), referencing Montessori's *Spontaneous Activity in Education* (reprinted as *The Advanced Montessori Method I*), Oxford: Clio Press, 1991 (originally 1918) and R. C. Roberts and W. J. Wood, *Intellectual Virtues: An Essay in Regulative Epistemology* (Oxford: Oxford University Press, 2007). Later Frierson continues, "Moreover, Montessori's *ethics* emphasizes respect for and solidarity with others, which require interpersonal humility."
48. Frierson argues that Montessori's epistemic humility is *intrinsically* epistemic as a virtue and that this has distinct advantages over contemporary virtue epistemologists who tend rather to see epistemic humility as only *contingently* epistemic, and essentially interpersonal.

6

How to Be Open-Minded: Ask Good Questions (and Listen to the Answers)

Lani Watson

In 2002, Daniella Young, aged just fifteen, navigated her way out of an infamous cult at that time known as the Children of God.[1] She writes about her experiences with uninhibited honesty, providing an insight into her early life inside the cult and her journey since leaving, first graduating from high school and college, and subsequently serving in the US army. Young's story is extraordinary for many reasons, not least of all for her account of a childhood characterized by extreme physical, psychological, and epistemic isolation, and for the courage it undoubtedly took to leave everything behind at such a young age. It is also the story of an exceptional capacity for open-mindedness in the face of apparently overwhelming odds against the development or exercise of the virtue. As such, Young's story, and those of many others who have spoken about leaving cults, can serve as valuable inspiration and instruction for a philosophical examination of open-mindedness.

I draw on Young's story in what follows in order to address the principal "how-to" challenge associated with open-mindedness, reflected in the chapter's title, namely, *how to be open-minded*. In other words, I am concerned with advancing strategies for exercising and cultivating the virtue of open-mindedness. Note that this is a self-consciously "how to" chapter, by which I mean that my focus is on the practical cultivation and exercise of open-mindedness, leaving aside important theoretical questions (many of which are addressed elsewhere in this volume). These include the question of what open-mindedness is, the

Lani Watson, *How to Be Open-Minded: Ask Good Questions (and Listen to the Answers)* In: *The Virtue of Open-Mindedness and Perspective.* Edited by: Wayne D. Riggs, Oxford University Press. © Oxford University Press 2025. DOI: 10.1093/9780190080723.003.0007

140 THE VIRTUE OF OPEN-MINDEDNESS

question of when to be open-minded, and the question of why it is (or isn't) good to be open-minded. I draw on the existing literature for an account of open-mindedness and believe that consideration of the principal how-to challenge of open-mindedness naturally intersects with the wider debate and can serve to helpfully inform it.

My central claim is that open-mindedness can be exercised and cultivated in the form of good questioning. I have argued elsewhere that good questioning is an important, perhaps even essential, component of the intellectually virtuous life (Watson 2019, 2020, 2022a, 2022b), and that teaching the skill of good questioning is a practical and effective pedagogical strategy for cultivating a range of intellectual virtues, including inquisitiveness, attentiveness, intellectual humility, intellectual autonomy, and intellectual courage (Watson 2016, 2018, 2020). This chapter contributes to the broader project of highlighting the significance of good questioning for intellectually virtuous character by extending the case to the virtue of open-mindedness; also, it illuminates a practical strategy for cultivating open-mindedness with broad applications in intellectual character education more generally.

In Section 2, I characterize the key concepts, namely, open-mindedness and good questioning. In Section 2, I argue that open-mindedness can be exercised in the form of good questioning. In Section 3, I draw some conclusions concerning the distinct "how-to" challenge of how to cultivate open-mindedness. Ultimately, I contend that one can both exercise and cultivate open-mindedness by asking good questions (and listening to the answers.)[2]

1 Open-Mindedness and Good Questioning

In her account of life as a member of the Children of God (COG), Young describes the extreme religious and epistemic control that she grew up with: "At 14, I had never set foot inside a school and was not allowed to read anything but the King James Bible or COG religious texts." The Children of God was founded by self-proclaimed prophetic leader, David Berg, who foregrounded the "looming spectre of the Apocalypse" to control the cult's substantial, international following. Such extensive control involved excessive and enforced isolation from

HOW TO BE OPEN-MINDED   141

the outside world. Young explains: "All my life I had been taught that police were out to get me, that schools taught nothing but lies, and that all Americans were evil." How, then, did the fifteen-year-old Young see past the fear-driven belief-system that encompassed everything she "knew," to a truth and a world beyond?

Without doubt, the answer to this question is complex, and Young sheds much light on this in her own words. She does not herself cite her extraordinary teenage capacity for open-mindedness as a causal factor but it seems plausible that this played a role. Indeed, it is perhaps easy to underestimate how central a role the virtue of open-mindedness plays in cases such as this. In order to appreciate this role we must begin with an account of open-mindedness (1.1). I will then provide an account of good questioning (1.2), to lay the groundwork for the argument, in Section II, that good questioning can be a form of open-mindedness. In fact, I will argue that good questioning can be a powerful form of open-mindedness allowing all of us, like Young, to see beyond the world as we "know" it, and test the boundaries of many of our most strongly-held (or strongly-enforced) beliefs.

1.1 What Is Open-Mindedness?

To begin, I assume that open-mindedness can be accurately characterized as an intellectual virtue, within the contemporary virtue epistemology tradition. This is broadly uncontentious. As Riggs (2010) comments in an early contribution to the study of open-mindedness, it appears paradigmatically on lists of intellectual virtues compiled by virtue epistemologists. Indeed, he notes, "It is striking how often open-mindedness is at the very top of that list." (p.173) What precisely makes open-mindedness an intellectual virtue is moderately more contentious. Carter and Gordon (2014) interrogate this question in some depth and highlight several puzzles for accounts of open-mindedness that explicate its status as an intellectual virtue in terms of its relation to truth. Nonetheless, even Carter and Gordon are unwilling to adopt a revisionist line that would deny open-mindedness the status of an intellectual virtue. Rather, they argue, these puzzles "give us reason enough to abandon what is otherwise a deeply entrenched

142 THE VIRTUE OF OPEN-MINDEDNESS

picture of the role of epistemic evaluations in epistemology" (p.218). For Carter and Gordon, the status of open-mindedness as an intellectual virtue is rendered simply too intuitive to deny, and many others agree. How, then, should we characterize the intellectual virtue of open-mindedness?

I adopt Jason Baehr's (2011) account of open-mindedness and use this as a foundation for the arguments that I advance in the following sections. Baehr's account is as follows:

> An open-minded person is characteristically (a) willing and (within limits) able (b) to transcend a default cognitive standpoint (c) in order to take up or take seriously the merits of (d) a distinct cognitive standpoint. (Baehr, 2011, p. 202)

In his detailed discussion of open-mindedness, Baehr (2011) develops and defends this account in light of two alternatives, which he terms the "conflict" and "adjudication" models of open-mindedness. Baehr argues that any account of open-mindedness must encompass cases in which no conflict or adjudication of beliefs is required. Rather, a person can be open-minded when they are, for instance, attempting to follow, understand, or comprehend some new or challenging subject matter, or where they have to imagine or conceive of possibilities and alternatives.

Baehr (2011) maintains that the "conceptual core" of open-mindedness, in all these cases, is a kind of detachment or transcendence: "In each case, a person *departs* or *detaches* from, he or she *moves beyond* or *transcends*, a certain default or privileged cognitive standpoint" (p. 199, emphasis original). This ability to transcend a default or privileged cognitive standpoint is essential to the exercise of virtuous open-mindedness. It ensures that, even absent the need for conflict resolution or adjudication among beliefs, the open-minded person will not simply accept the status quo of her belief system, including any biases or prejudices. Open-mindedness is exercised both by positively opening up one's mind and, sometimes, by merely not closing it (Baehr, 2011, p.201).

I will not defend Baehr's account of open-mindedness here. It is, I think, compelling and has traction in the wider literature. As such,

I am comfortable drawing on this account as a foundation for the discussion that follows. That said, while I focus on some specifics of Baehr's account, it is worth noting that the central contention of this chapter—that open-mindedness can be exercised in the form of good questioning—can be equally well established in light of alternative accounts of open-mindedness, including those of Hare (2003), Adler (2004), Riggs (2010), Spiegel (2012), and Kwong (2016). There is not space to develop an argument in relation to the specifics of each of these accounts, but the overall picture will, I think, be sufficient to establish its broad compatibility with them all. I will draw on these accounts in places to illustrate this and, in general, I regard it as an advantage that the argument is compatible with different views of open-mindedness. Likewise, I remain neutral on the questions of when and whether one should be open or closed-minded and so the argument is compatible with views that regard open-mindedness as vicious in certain contexts (Fantl 2018) and closed-mindedness as virtuous in certain contexts (Battaly 2018).

1.2 What Is Good Questioning?

My central claim is that one can exercise open-mindedness in the form of good questioning. In order to substantiate this, an account of good questioning is required in addition to the account of open-mindedness already adopted. I have developed and defended an account of good questioning in several places (Watson 2018, 2019, 2022b). I will offer an outline here sufficient for elucidating the relationship between open-mindedness and good questioning, and specifically, for establishing the central claim.

The practice of questioning is both familiar and commonplace. *Good* questioning, however, is a complex and dynamic skill and is, therefore, naturally less ubiquitous. Nonetheless, we often know good questioning when we see it. Some people have a knack for asking just the right questions at just the right time, and one might wonder how they do it. To offer an account of good questioning, I first take questioning to be a particular kind of act; the act of information-seeking. When one engages in questioning (good or bad), one is

144   THE VIRTUE OF OPEN-MINDEDNESS

fundamentally engaged in seeking information.[3] As good questioning is a skill, converting questioning into good questioning means seeking information skillfully. This elevates good questioning above mere information-seeking in two ways. When we engage in the skill of good questioning, we do not simply seek information; rather, we *competently* seek information that is *worth having*. I explicate these conditions in turn.

First, good questioning requires seeking worthwhile information. This means attending to the "what" of the question; what information is the questioner attempting to find out? I call this "what" the content of a question. This content comprises the target information that the questioner is seeking when asking a question; it is "what" they are trying to find out. This feature of good questioning entails that the good questioner is not simply trying to find out any and all information. Rather, she is seeking information that is worthwhile, relevant, or important in some sense.

There are two basic senses in which information can be considered worthwhile in the context of good questioning. In the first sense, good questioning excludes cases of trivial or disvaluable information-seeking. The good questioner does not waste time seeking information she does not need or want, nor does she seek information that will be actively harmful to herself or others. Thus, worthwhile information-seeking is partly determined by a questioner's ability to identify information that will advance her personal epistemic interests in service of achieving certain goals, and partly by her ability to judge what information may inhibit those goals and/or be actively harmful to herself or others.

In the second sense, worthwhile information-seeking requires the good questioner not only to avoid seeking certain information but actively to seek out relevant, valuable, or significant information. The good questioner will seek only the information that she needs or wants and, in doing so, will avoid any irrelevant, insignificant, or harmful information that is also available to her. It is not hard to see that some instances of questioning falter precisely in virtue of the questioner's failure to seek out relevant, valuable, or significant information; in short, information that is worth having. Thus, the skill of good questioning requires the questioner to engage in

HOW TO BE OPEN-MINDED 145

worthwhile information-seeking, both through the avoidance of trivial, disvaluable, or harmful information and in the acquisition of information that is relevant, valuable, or significant.[4]

Second, good questioning requires seeking worthwhile information competently. Competently seeking information requires attending to the "who," "when," "where," and "how" of the question; who is being asked, when and where they are being asked, and how they are being asked. I call these the contextual and communicative components of good questioning. In addition to targeting worthwhile content, these further components reveal the dynamic complexity of good questioning as both an epistemic and practical skill. One's questions can misfire in numerous subtle and interconnected ways. One may go wrong by asking the wrong person or source, for example. Likewise, a question may miss its target because it is badly timed or the situation in which it is asked is misjudged. Even more subtly, the tone or delivery of a question can affect its reception and effectiveness, even when the information sought is worthwhile. All of these factors can prevent a person from engaging in good questioning.

Notably, competent information-seeking does not permit information that is acquired by accident or luck. On the other hand, it does not always require that the information sought is in fact acquired. Rather, in certain circumstances one may competently seek information without actually acquiring it. Good questioning requires competent information-seeking but successfully acquiring information is neither necessary nor sufficient. To summarize, then, questioning is good in virtue of competent and worthwhile information-seeking. A good questioner competently seeks worthwhile information.

We now have characterizations of the two key concepts arising in the chapter's central claim that open-mindedness can be exercised in the form of good questioning. With these in play, I will turn to the how-to challenge expressed at the outset: how to be open-minded. In fact, in line with the central claim, I reframe this challenge in terms of the *exercise* of the virtue. This is a minor point but the latter, I think, better captures the sense in which open-mindedness, like all virtues, is dynamic and active, involving identifiable behaviors and requiring continual practice. It is not enough simply *to be* open-minded, one must do certain things and act in certain ways. Or, more accurately, *being*

146   THE VIRTUE OF OPEN-MINDEDNESS

open-minded is not a passive state, but involves actively *exercising* the virtue. With this in mind, I will argue that open-mindedness can be exercised in the form of good questioning.

2 How to Exercise Open-Mindedness

In her account, Young refers to members of COG as "unquestioning followers."[5] She emphasizes the obedient compliance expected of cult members as both children and adults and, at several points, identifies a link between this obedience and the absence or prohibition of questioning. She comments, for example, "We didn't question the Prophet when he said that periods of forced isolation were to help us commune with Jesus."[6] According to Young's account, this unquestioning mindset inhibited interrogation and critical evaluation of both the cult's teachings and the authority of its senior figures, principally, its self-appointed "prophet."

The unwillingness or inability to ask questions in this setting is disconcerting for many reasons. Exploratory, at times relentless, questioning is often exhibited by young children and is a familiar stage in their cognitive development. Spirited, sometimes challenging, questions are a hallmark of adolescence. Most of us continue to ask questions about the world around us and our place within it throughout our lives, with varying degrees of curiosity and persistence. To actively inhibit this natural instinct, in both children and adults, suggests a deep manipulation of intellectual character and, arguably, amounts to a serious violation of epistemic rights (Watson 2021b). At any rate, to be described as unquestioning is not, typically, taken to be a positive reflection of intellectual character, indicating a lack of thoughtful engagement or a blind acceptance of the status quo. It can also, for these reasons, be indicative of a closed mind.

This connection between the unquestioning mindset that Young describes and that of closed-mindedness is, I think, relatively intuitive. One feature of being an "unquestioning follower" is surely having a closed mind to alternative realities outside the cult and its leadership. Likewise, it is not hard to appreciate a converse intuitive connection between open-mindedness and questioning. Indeed, I take it to be relatively uncontentious that, in everyday life as in cults, an unwillingness or inability to ask questions about a given topic can indicate that a person has a closed mind on that topic and, conversely, that a willingness and ability to ask questions can indicate that a person has an open mind on that topic. These intuitive connections serve as a starting point for establishing a conceptually tighter relationship between open-mindedness and questioning (2.1), and, in due course, for the claim that open-mindedness can be exercised in the form of good questioning (2.2 and 2.3).

2.1 The Relationship between Open-Mindedness and Questioning

In order to reach the conclusion of Section II, it will be instructive to first explicate the relationship between open-mindedness and questioning *simpliciter* (before elucidating what is meant by "form of" and introducing the qualifier "good"). Here, then, I argue that there is a conceptually tight relationship between open-mindedness and questioning *simpliciter*. By "conceptually tight" I mean that the relationship between these concepts does not merely consist in a superficial likeness or an incidental correlation. Rather these concepts share central features in common, such that there exists significant conceptual overlap between them. To see this, we can return to the account of open-mindedness outlined above.

To recap, on Baehr's (2011) account:

> An open-minded person is characteristically (a) willing and (within limits) able (b) to transcend a default cognitive standpoint (c) in order to take up or take seriously the merits of (d) a distinct cognitive standpoint. (Baehr, 2011, p. 202)

Each of the conditions (a)–(d) makes a discrete contribution to Baehr's characterization of open-mindedness. Close examination of these reveals a tight conceptual link between open-mindedness and questioning. In particular, I will examine conditions (a), (b), and (d).[7]

148 THE VIRTUE OF OPEN-MINDEDNESS

To begin, condition (a) states that the open-minded person is "willing and (within limits) able." While this condition makes little sense on its own, it is worth clarifying with reference to the origins of these requirements within the virtue epistemology literature. In her seminal work, Linda Zagzebski (1996) argues that all of the intellectual virtues feature two basic components: a motivation component and a skill (or success) component. That the open-minded person must be both *willing* and *able* reflects these two components of the virtue. Naturally, however, they are not sufficient on their own; we must also understand precisely *what* the open-minded person is willing and able to do. Conditions (b)–(d) are the details that fill out this picture.

Building on condition (a), condition (b) states that the open-minded person must be willing and able to "transcend a default cognitive standpoint." Recall that Baehr (2011) identifies this ability to "detach from" or "transcend" a default cognitive standpoint as the conceptual core of open-mindedness. Condition (b) is thus central to his characterization of the virtue and it is important to understand what is meant by this notion of transcendence. Baehr elucidates this in his article (2011, pp. 200–202), describing it as a "willingness to consider things from the other side" (p. 200), an "intellectual 'opening'... of one's present cognitive perspective" (p. 200), an ability "to identify or conceive of explanations that would otherwise be out of reach" (p. 200) or to "move back and forth between the positions in question" (p. 201), and to "resist the temptation to make a hasty generalization" (p. 201).

These details paint a coherent and relatively tangible picture of the notion of cognitive transcendence that Baehr has in mind. One might take issue with specific aspects of this picture or find the analysis somewhat imprecise, but I take it that these details, and the wider discussion that frames them, provide a reasonable insight into what Baehr *means* when he speaks of transcendence as the conceptual core of open-mindedness. In particular, for present purposes, it is important to note that Baehr is describing a process or activity rather than a fixed state; the conceptual core of open-mindedness, for Baehr, consists in the *activity of transcending* as opposed to the state of transcendence. That said, it is not always clear from this picture *how* one engages in the activity of transcending and thereby *how* one transcends a cognitive standpoint. This is my task, rather than Baehr's, and it is here that the conceptually tight relationship between open-mindedness and questioning emerges most clearly.

Running conditions (a) and (b) together provides the best insight into this. Put simply, one can be willing and able to transcend a default cognitive standpoint by engaging in questioning. This is because questioning typically involves recognizing that one does not have all the information one needs or wants. It requires one to identify a gap in one's knowledge or understanding and constitutes an attempt to fill that gap. This is likewise required in order to transcend a cognitive standpoint (default or otherwise). If one believes that one's cognitive standpoint on a given topic includes or is based on all of the information required to hold that standpoint, then there is little cause to transcend it. One may, in fact, fail to notice the standpoint at all. Noticing, or at least considering, the possibility that one *may not* have all the information to support one's position on a topic is what enables one, in the first instance, to move beyond it. Moreover, questioning does not consist in merely recognizing that one does not have all the information that one needs or wants. As with Baehr's notion of transcending, questioning is a process or activity rather than a fixed state. As such, when one in engages in questioning, one engages in an activity that involves recognizing that one is missing information and acting on that recognition by seeking to acquire the information. This is at least one way to transcend a default cognitive standpoint.

Imagine, for example, that I believe that human-induced climate change is happening and, in addition, I believe that I have all the information I need to hold this position. Under these circumstances, I am unlikely to ask the question, "Is climate change caused by humans?" Similarly, imagine that I believe the apocalypse is imminent and, in addition, I believe that I have all the information I need to hold this position. Again, under these circumstances, I am unlikely to ask the question, "Is the apocalypse imminent?" In both cases, I am unlikely to ask because I believe that I already have all the information I need to support my position. As such, I am unlikely to transcend my position, and thus I am unlikely to exercise open-mindedness.

However, imagine that, despite this, I actually do ask whether climate change is caused by humans or whether the apocalypse imminent (and that my questions are sincere, as opposed to rhetorical).

150 THE VIRTUE OF OPEN-MINDEDNESS

I think these questions can be viewed as paradigmatic instances of what Baehr (2011) describes as the "intellectual 'opening' . . . of one's present cognitive perspective" (p. 2 00). They exhibit a concrete "willingness to consider things from the other side" (p. 200). As such, by asking questions under these conditions, I am engaging in the activity of transcending my cognitive standpoint, according to Baehr's characterization of this activity. This activity constitutes the conceptual core of open-mindedness according to Baehr. Thus, the conceptual overlap between open-mindedness and questioning appears significant.[8]

This becomes even clearer when we look at condition (d) in Baehr's account. This condition highlights the significance of distinct alternatives in the exercise of open-mindedness. The open-minded person must not merely transcend a default cognitive standpoint; she must also be willing and able to consider alternative standpoints. Naturally, these things are closely bound such that the act of transcending a cognitive standpoint without thereby considering alternatives seems odd. Nonetheless, it is helpful to consider condition (d) in its own right in order to appreciate the significance of alternatives in identifying the conceptual overlap between open-mindedness and questioning.

Questioning by its nature posits the existence of alternatives. When one asks a question, one is (at least implicitly) aware of the existence of a range of possible answers. If this were not the case, it would not make sense to ask. One can appreciate this in its simplest form with yes/no questions. When I ask "Is it raining?" I am (among other things) positing the existence of two possible answers, "yes" and "no," and seeking information to determine which is correct. If I already know that it is raining, then I do not need to consider these alternatives and so I do not need to seek the relevant information. As such, I do not need to ask. There is here a natural analogy with treasure-seeking. Seeking treasure on a desert island involves putting one's shovel in the sand in different places and digging with the hope of reward. In other words, it involves trying out a series of alternatives. If one already knows where the treasure is, one does not need to posit the existence of alternative locations, and thus one does not need to seek (one just needs to dig in the right location). Seeking, whether it be treasure or information, implies the existence of a range of alternatives that one is not yet in a position to rule out.

HOW TO BE OPEN-MINDED 151

It is worth underlining the significance of this feature of questioning in order to fully appreciate its relationship to the conceptual core of open-mindedness, according to Baehr's account. As I said earlier, it is odd to consider condition (d) as distinct from conditions (a) and (b) in the account. This is because it is odd to detach one's awareness of distinct alternatives from the activity of transcending one's default cognitive standpoint. What would it mean to engage in the activity of transcending a cognitive standpoint if one was not simultaneously aware of the existence of alternatives. In much the same way, it is odd to detach one's awareness of alternatives from the activity of questioning. Indeed, one would be very unlikely to engage in the activity of questioning (sincerely) without an awareness of alternatives.

Return to the questions asked earlier: "Is climate change caused by humans?" and "Is the apocalypse imminent?" Asking these questions posits the existence of a range of possible answers (in both cases, "yes" and "no"). However remote one or another of those answers may seem, asking the questions (sincerely) is a way of acknowledging the existence of alternatives that one is not yet in a position to rule out. Asking these questions can therefore be viewed as instances of what Baehr (2011) describes as the ability "to identify or conceive of explanations that would otherwise be out of reach" (p. 200) and to "move back and forth between the positions in question" (p. 201). As such, by asking questions, one is engaging in the activity of transcending a cognitive standpoint in light of a distinct cognitive standpoint, according to Baehr's characterization of this activity. This is essential for exercising open-mindedness, according to Baehr, and thus we see once again significant conceptual overlap between open-mindedness and questioning.

Indeed, one might even argue that the overlap is substantial enough to allow for a direct switch in Baehr's account, replacing the word "transcend" in condition (b) with the word "question": to be open-minded is to be willing and able to *question* a default cognitive standpoint (and so on). This would have the advantage of removing the somewhat opaque notion of transcendence and replacing it with the, at least prima facie, clearer and more accessible notion of questioning. Moreover, this switch would build a response to the "how-to" challenge directly into the characterization itself given that it seems likely

152 THE VIRTUE OF OPEN-MINDEDNESS

that we know how to question at least more intuitively than we know how to "transcend." I will not extend the case in favor of this strategy here—it is certainly a stronger claim than the one I am arguing for in this chapter. Nonetheless, I make the point in order to underline the significant overlapping conceptual terrain that exists between these concepts. This suggests that questioning can itself be a *form of* open-mindedness.

2.2 Questioning as a Form of Open-Mindedness

What does it mean to say that questioning can be a *form of* open-mindedness. To begin, a point of clarification is needed. By "form of" open-mindedness, I mean that open-mindedness can be "realized" or "manifested" as questioning—in other words, it can *take the form of* questioning. On a slightly different reading, this phrasing could be interpreted as signifying something like a "class" or "type" of open-mindedness. This is not my intended meaning. Rather, I mean to capture how open-mindedness can and does manifest in the world or, perhaps more simply, what it *looks like*—its form. When I say that questioning can be a form of open-mindedness, then, I mean that being open-minded sometimes looks like good questioning.

The preceding section has already provided some grounds for this. As noted, I take it to be relatively uncontentious that a willingness and ability to ask questions about a given topic can be indicative of an open mind on that topic. This is a simple but useful point. It suggests that, in certain circumstances, we can and do infer open-mindedness when we *see* questioning. Take, for example, an utterance like "her questions indicate that she is open-minded to the suggestion." There is nothing prima facie unusual or unreasonable about such an utterance. Of course, the content of the questions and their sincerity would need to be interrogated in order to establish whether such an utterance was accurate and fair, but, in general, there is nothing odd or objectionable about the inference being expressed. This is because there is nothing odd or objectionable about the idea that open-mindedness sometimes looks like or takes the form of questioning. One might use similarly descriptive words like "show," "express," or "demonstrate," as in, "her

HOW TO BE OPEN-MINDED   153

questions demonstrate that she is open-minded about this" or "the fact that he is asking questions shows that he at least has an open mind." Utterances like this are not odd or disjointed. Rather, they appear to express the particular sense in which questioning can, in certain cases, look like or take the form of questioning.

Further to this, and drawing on Baehr's (2011) characterization of open-mindedness, I have argued that the relationship between open-mindedness and questioning is conceptually tight. More specifically, I have argued that the conceptual core of open-mindedness, according to Baehr's account, can be realized or manifested as questioning. Indeed, I have suggested that the cognitive transcendence Baehr places at the heart of his account could itself be accurately characterized as nothing more than questioning. Again, I am not defending the latter, stronger claim here, but I do think that the intuitive strength of this suggestion rests largely on the kinds of considerations about the nature of the relationship between open-mindedness and questioning presented earlier. How do we identify, recognize, or *see* cognitive transcendence? How does it manifest in the course of a conversation, or, for that matter, in our own private cogitations? My answer: often, if not typically, *in the form of questioning.*

Notably, we can also look beyond Baehr's account to other prominent expositions of open-mindedness in the literature in order to elucidate the sense in which questioning can be a form of open-mindedness. Jonathan Adler (2004) posits that open-mindedness is "a second-order (or 'meta') attitude toward one's beliefs as believed, and not just toward the specific proposition believed" (p. 130). This attitude consists in "an appreciation of our fallibility" (p. 130). For Adler, this appreciation is an essential characteristic of open-mindedness. Likewise, Riggs (2010) highlights the centrality of this appreciation. Inspired by Adler, Riggs says, "To be open-minded is to be aware of one's fallibility as a believer, and to be willing to acknowledge the possibility that anytime one believes something, *it is possible that one is wrong*" (Riggs, 2010, p. 180, emphasis original).

What does this appreciation or acknowledgment look like? How does it manifest in our conversations with others or our personal cogitations? Again, I think it often, if not typically, takes the form of questioning. Questions, after all, are premised on ignorance. We ask

154   THE VIRTUE OF OPEN-MINDEDNESS

questions precisely when we notice that we are missing some piece of information, knowledge, or understanding.[9] I do not, for example, ask whether my name is Lucy or whether I live in Manhattan unless I am suffering from some kind of memory loss that has rendered this information unavailable to me. If I do ask these questions, it is very probably because I do not know the answers, or feel uncertain or doubtful. In other words, I am aware of the possibility that I may be wrong about my name and the city in which I live. In asking, I simultaneously acknowledge and communicate this uncertainty and doubt, exposing the fact that I am not sure what my name is or where I live. Again, I do not ask these questions in my normal life because I am already very confident about the answers.

As such, questioning represents a somewhat paradigmatic instance of the appreciation of fallibility that both Adler and Riggs regard as central to open-mindedness. If I ask whether my name is Lucy, I signal that I am open to the possibility that it is not. The fact that I have never asked whether my name is Lani suggests (albeit somewhat implicitly or passively) that I am closed to the possibility that it is not. The same goes for the examples discussed previously. If I ask "Is climate change caused by humans?" I signal that I am open to the possibility it is not. Likewise, if Young had asked "Is the apocalypse imminent?" in the context of the Children of God, this would have sent a strong and provocative signal that she was open to the possibility that it is not. The question automatically raises the possibility that the accepted view is wrong, suggesting an otherwise unacknowledged (and in Young's case unwelcome) fallibility.

Questioning is, then, one way that the fallibility central to open-mindedness can be realized or manifested. This manifestation is important for accurately characterizing open-mindedness. Adler (2004), for example, offers the compelling analogy of a widget factory, to furnish his account of open-mindedness as meta-level appreciation of one's fallibility as a believer. In the analogy, there is a quality assurance manager in the factory systematically checking individual widgets for defects, despite having a belief that none of the individual widgets are defective. Adler notes that the manager is nonetheless justified (indeed obligated) to check at least some of the widgets, in case anything goes wrong. The widgets in the analogy represent individual beliefs and the quality assurance manager represents the open-minded believer, duly ensuring the overall quality of her belief-system, despite believing that none of her individual beliefs are false.

Somewhat overlooked in this analogy is the activity itself, which Adler refers to simply as "checking." Checking is in play both in Adler's initial description of the analogy and when he uses it to elucidate open-mindedness: the quality assurance manager checks the widgets and the open-minded person checks her beliefs. Crucially, without this active checking neither the quality assurance manager nor the open-minded person would be "doing their job." In other words, a meta-level appreciation of fallibility alone will not assure the quality of the widgets—the manager must act on this by actually checking the widgets. Likewise, the open-minded person must actually check her beliefs.

In the case of open-mindedness, I think this active checking can be accurately construed as questioning. At least some, if not all of the time, checking one's beliefs consists in questioning them. Indeed, much like Baehr's central notion of cognitive transcendence, one might plausibly replace "checking" with "questioning" in Adler's exposition of open-mindedness. Checking the individual factory widgets is analogous to questioning one's individual beliefs. Questioning, then, is plausibly the *activity* at the heart of Adler's account of open-mindedness.

Notably, Riggs (2010) draws attention to the significance of activities and behaviors for open-mindedness. Rather than adopting Adler's (2004) account of open-mindedness as a meta-level attitude wholesale, Riggs takes it as a starting point for his own account:

> This attitude alone will not constitute open-mindedness. The attitude must be efficacious in our cognitive lives. It must intrude upon our habits of thought consistently and productively to produce the cognitive and overt "behaviour" typical of those we take to exemplify open-mindedness. (Riggs, 2010, p. 182)

In other words, Riggs seeks to move beyond the characterization of open-mindedness as a mere attitude. Rather, he insists, open-mindedness requires behaving and acting in certain ways. Again, I argue that this activity—whether exemplified in overt behavior or

156   THE VIRTUE OF OPEN-MINDEDNESS

internal "habits of thought"—often, if not typically, takes the form of questioning.

A final prominent account of open-mindedness also helps to make this case. Jack Kwong (2016) characterizes open-mindedness in terms of engagement. He says, "A person is open-minded when she is willing to engage with a novel idea, that is, when she is willing to make room for it in her cognitive space and to give it serious consideration" (p. 85). Kwong argues that this account of open-mindedness improves on all three of the alternatives discussed above (Baehr 2011, Adler 2004, and Riggs 2010). I remain neutral on that point. Rather, as with these alternatives, one can ask what this engagement looks like. What form does it take in both our conversations with others and our personal cogitations? Often, if not typically, I think it takes the form of questioning. This is what "willingness to engage with a novel idea" and "willingness to make room for it in cognitive space" look like when translated into overt actions and behaviors. Indeed, questioning is perhaps a paradigmatic form of engagement. In other words, if open-mindedness is engagement, then it often, perhaps paradigmatically, takes the form of questioning.

I have thus argued that open-mindedness can take the form of questioning and have demonstrated the compatibility of this claim with several prominent accounts of the virtue. In Baehr's (2011) terms, I have argued that transcending a cognitive standpoint often (perhaps always) takes the form of questioning that standpoint (in light of alternatives). Turning to Adler (2004) and Riggs (2010), I have argued that an appreciation of one's fallibility often, if not typically, takes the form of questioning. In Kwong's (2016) terms, I have argued that engagement often, perhaps paradigmatically takes the form of questioning. In other words, it is no coincidence that we intuitively recognize a connection between open-mindedness and questioning. There is significant conceptual overlap between open-mindedness and questioning evidenced by the fact that questioning shares central features with not just one but several prominent accounts of open-mindedness in the literature. Open-mindedness is not a mere attitude or static state—it involves both overt and internal activities and behaviors. These can, and I think often do, take the form of questioning. Thus, I contend, open-mindedness can be exercised in the form of questioning.

2.3 Good Questioning as a Form of Open-Mindedness

We are now most of the way toward establishing the central claim of the chapter. That claim, however, includes a qualifier not yet defended. Specifically, not all questioning amounts to open-mindedness; rather, it must be *good* questioning. I offered an account of good questioning in 1.1 and we can now return to that account to see how it maps onto open-mindedness. Recall that good questioning requires both competent and worthwhile information-seeking: the good questioner competently seeks worthwhile information. This account contains two conditions that elevate good questioning above mere questioning: "competency" and "worthwhileness." Taking these conditions in reverse, I will demonstrate how they map onto open-mindedness, thereby underscoring the significance of the qualifier for the overall argument.

In the first place, then, recall that seeking worthwhile information means attending to the "what," or the content, of a question: the information the questioner is trying to find out. The good questioner is not simply trying to find out any and all information. Rather, she is seeking information that is worthwhile in the senses discussed earlier. Importantly, this is also true of the open-minded person. Being open-minded does not amount to accepting any and all information; rather, it requires a high degree of selectivity.

Adler (2004) makes this point compellingly. He emphasizes that to be open-minded with respect to every one of our beliefs would be a vast and impossible task, as well as a significant waste of our limited cognitive resources: "In fact, given the vastness of our beliefs, open-mindedness will serve its primary purpose only if we are highly selective about what to be open-minded about" (p. 134). This is borne out in the analogy of the widget factory. The quality assurance officer cannot check every single widget for defects, that would be an enormous waste of time and resource. Rather, she selects only certain widgets for checking. Likewise, the open-minded person must be selective about checking—or questioning—her beliefs. It is this selectivity that makes her open-minded, as opposed to, say, gullible.

Notably, Adler is here addressing the "how-to" question with which I am also concerned. He argues that we need self-knowledge in order

158 THE VIRTUE OF OPEN-MINDEDNESS

to be highly selective about our beliefs and so to determine which ones to be open-minded about. Unlike the quality assurance officer in the widget factory, we cannot simply rely on a randomized system to check our beliefs. We should, for example, be more open-minded about controversial beliefs, than about the products of perception (that the sky is blue, etc.). Most important, Adler maintains that open-mindedness requires self-knowledge about our prejudices and biases (a point also stressed by Riggs (2010) and Hare (2011)). Notably, this self-knowledge is often realized in the form of good questioning. We *question* our position on a particular topic in order to determine whether it has been influenced by an implicit bias or unconscious prejudice. Open-mindedness demands this. However, one does not (and cannot) question one's position with respect to every single thing that one believes. *Both* open-mindedness and good questioning prohibit this because both open-mindedness and good questioning involve being highly selective about content.

Open-mindedness and good questioning thus share an evaluative element, which questioning simpliciter lacks. One is not required to consider whether the information one is after is worthwhile in order merely to ask a question. Likewise, believing everything one reads in the *National Enquirer* without hesitation may be regarded as some form of openness—say gullibility—but it does not amount to open-mindedness. The same element of selectivity is required in both cases. One must be selective about content to elevate mere questioning to good questioning and one must be selective about content to elevate mere openness to open-mindedness. This evaluative element highlights the significance of the qualifier "good" in the claim that I am defending.

However, this is not all there is to good questioning. Alongside worthwhileness there is also the competency condition. The good questioner must competently seek worthwhile information. Recall that this means attending to the "who," "when," "where," and "how" of questioning: the contextual and communicative components. Thus, the good questioner does not ask questions at random times and places, or of random sources, or in a confusing manner. Rather, she pays attention to sources that are likely to have the information she needs and seeks it at an appropriate time and place using terms

HOW TO BE OPEN-MINDED   159

that will be easily understood. All of this adds up to her competency in seeking information via questioning.

As with the worthwhileness condition, this competency condition also holds for open-mindedness. The open-minded person must also pay attention to her sources and the context and manner in which she is adopting or rejecting particular beliefs. Again, being open-minded does not amount to accepting any and all information from any and all sources. Rather, it requires a high degree of selectivity. In this case, selectivity about the sources of one's beliefs, as opposed to the beliefs themselves. As Adler (2004) puts it:

> The need for high selectively in order for open-mindedness to be worthwhile applies to *how* one is open-minded, and not only to *what* one is open-minded toward. The primary question is what sources to attend to in checking on one's beliefs. (Adler, 2004, p. 135)

Again, open-mindedness and good questioning share an evaluative element here, which questioning simpliciter lacks. One is not required to consider who, when, where, or how one asks a question in order merely to ask it. This is required only in order to do it well—in other words, to engage in good questioning. Likewise, consulting the *National Enquirer* for all of one's beliefs may amount to some form of openness but it does not amount to open-mindedness. The same selectivity is required in both cases. One must be selective about context to engage in good questioning and one must be selective about context to be considered open-minded.

Notice that this evaluative element is not simply shared by open-mindedness and good questioning but in fact binds them together. To see this, take the questions I used earlier as examples: "Is climate change caused by humans?" and "Is the apocalypse imminent?" These questions stand or fall as good questions depending on the evaluative criteria set out above and captured by the worthwhileness and competency conditions. In particular, it is easy to see on reflection that these conditions are interdependent. Whether or not some information is worthwhile will almost certainly depend on the circumstances in which it is being sought. The question "Is climate change caused by humans?" was a good question several decades ago, when the evidence

160 THE VIRTUE OF OPEN-MINDEDNESS

was not conclusive and the answer was less clear. Now that the evidence weighs heavily in favor of the answer "yes," the question is, for the most part, not a good one and arguably, for the most part, a particularly bad one. Likewise, the question "Is the apocalypse imminent?" is, under non-cult-like circumstances, at best an odd one. But for Daniella Young, growing up in a setting where believing that the apocalypse is imminent is literally, gospel, this would arguably have been one of the best possible questions to ask.

Crucially, note that these judgments about the quality of the questions align with similar judgments that we might make about the open-mindedness of the asker. Taking into account what we know in 2022 about climate change, for instance, a person who today asks whether climate change is caused by humans may appear to be indicating a degree of climate skepticism, and thus *closed*-mindedness on this topic. Likewise, absent the cult-like circumstances of COG, asking whether a (vengeful-deity-induced) apocalypse is imminent may be a sign that the asker is failing to be appropriately selective about their beliefs and/or their sources and so, in this regard, falling short of open-mindedness. The details of course matter greatly but the simple point is that these kinds of alignments further support the more general alignment between good questioning and open-mindedness. As before, this evaluative element highlights the significance of the qualifier "good" in the claim that I am defending. Combining this with the argument in 2.1, we have arrived at the conclusion that open-mindedness can be exercised in the form of good questioning.

3 How to Cultivate Open-Mindedness

I hope by now that the reader is convinced of the above conclusion. Open-mindedness can indeed be exercised in the form of good questioning. In essence, this is my answer to the how-to challenge posed at the outset and reflected in the chapter's title. The challenge: how to be open-minded. The solution: ask good questions (and listen to the answers). I think this is a useful solution and one that intersects with other more squarely theoretical questions in the

HOW TO BE OPEN-MINDED   161

literature concerning open-mindedness, including questions about its nature and value.

That said, I will take this final section to highlight the distinctively practical significance of the claim that I have been defending. I am, after all, addressing an explicitly practical question. As such, my hope is that those in search of implementable strategies for exercising open-mindedness will find something concrete in the discussion of this chapter. If you find yourself closing down in a challenging conversation with someone you disagree with, and you want to resist that impulse, focus on asking good questions (and listening to the answers). If you find yourself struggling to understand a complex theorem or political situation because of preconceived ideas about how things are or should be, try formulating some good questions to uncover and challenge your assumptions. If you want to root out and avoid unconscious (or indeed conscious) bias and prejudice, ask questions about how and why such bias and prejudice may have set in. If you are brought up believing that the apocalypse is imminent, that schools teach lies, and that you are in the presence of a prophet . . . ask questions.

At just fourteen years old, Young devised her escape plan for leaving the Children of God:

> In an autocratic society, with no room for differences of opinion, where no questioning of authority is allowed and there is excommunication for anyone who dares to be different, my escape route soon became clear: I wouldn't have to run away if I could get them to kick me out.[10]

Young became actively defiant, flouting the strict isolation rules and seeking stimulus and experiences in the outside world. Such actions allowed her to question the authority of the cult leadership in a way that was otherwise prohibited. In a similar vein, one can imagine her asking questions about teachings in the religious texts she was exposed to, sending a strong signal that such teachings were not, at least in her mind, beyond doubt. Young does not describe this course of action in her account but it is not hard to imagine how effective it might have been as a strategy.

162   THE VIRTUE OF OPEN-MINDEDNESS

Indeed, this brings us to the question of how we can not only exercise open-mindedness, but actively cultivate it in ourselves and others. A classroom in which students are not allowed to ask questions about the content they are being taught, or anything else, for that matter, is a classroom in which the development of open-mindedness in students is likely to be inhibited. This is because, as I have argued, open-mindedness often, perhaps typically or even always, takes the form of good questioning. Consequently, without opportunities to question, students are missing out on opportunities to practice at least one prominent form of the virtue. The virtues, moreover, require practice and, through practice, the formation of habit—as Riggs (2010) puts it, "habits of thought" (p. 182). In the case of open-mindedness, one effective way to curtail the development of the virtue is to restrict the practice of questioning so that the habit cannot emerge.

Of course, the flipside to this is that one effective way to both exercise and cultivate open-mindedness is by practicing, and thus habituating, the skill of good questioning. This goes for others as well as ourselves. We can, in essence, teach open-mindedness by teaching good questioning. As well as being attractive in its simplicity, this strategy has the advantage of being relatively concrete and implementable. I have argued elsewhere that we can and should teach the skill of good questioning (Watson 2018, 2019, 2020). Effective pedagogical strategies for doing so have been tried and tested at scale, particularly via the Question Formulation Technique developed by the *Right Question Institute* (Rothstein and Santana, 2011). In their earliest years, children begin to ask provocative and unexpected questions, at home and at school. More than anything, teachers need to be equipped with the time and techniques simply to let this natural propensity flourish and mature. Again, we can and should teach students how to ask good questions in order to cultivate the virtue of open-mindedness.

That is not to say that doing so is not at times challenging and complex. But it is also undoubtedly, in my mind, a more pragmatic and achievable task than, for example, teaching students to transcend a cognitive standpoint, adopt a second-order attitude of fallibility toward their beliefs, or simply to "engage" without further concrete pedagogical instruction. I stress that proponents of the associated

HOW TO BE OPEN-MINDED   163

accounts of open-mindedness (Baehr, Adler, Riggs, Kwong) did not set themselves the explicitly practical task that I have taken on here, so this is not intended as a criticism of those accounts. Nonetheless, I draw the contrast in order to underline the comparably practical nature of the solution I have offered in service of efforts to cultivate open-mindedness. Indeed, this solution can serve to practically enhance theoretical accounts of open-mindedness. One might ask of each of these accounts how we can teach students to transcend a cognitive standpoint, to adopt a second-order attitude of fallibility toward their beliefs, or to engage in an open-minded way. In each case, the answer is by teaching them the skill of good questioning.

Hare (2009, 2011) is one scholar who has taken on the how-to challenge of cultivating open-mindedness more directly. This is not surprising given his focus on open-mindedness in education. In "Helping Open-Mindedness Flourish" (2011), Hare provides a rich account of the classroom (and broader educational) conditions that are required in order to cultivate open-mindedness. To my mind, Hare's ten recommendations constitute something more like the ideal background conditions for cultivating open-mindedness rather than concrete suggestions for pedagogical strategy—which is not to diminish their value. Certainly, the educational context that Young experienced in COG would have been transformed if such conditions had been realize, even minimally. Moreover, a small number of concrete suggestions are included in the discussion. Specifically, Hare (2011) notes: "In addition, we can develop the habit of raising the kinds of questions likely to detect baseless claims" (p.13).

In a separate article, Hare (2009) takes this suggestion further:

"Schooling must not only avoid indoctrination in every form but also help students to learn how to recognize and resist indoctrination and to develop their own independent judgement. This entails the nurturing of critical-thinking skills and the disposition to apply them. These aims of education and schooling need to be embedded in an approach to teaching that promotes discussion and inquiry in classrooms, encourages curiosity and wonder in students, welcomes questions from students that probe claims made by the teacher, and

164   THE VIRTUE OF OPEN-MINDEDNESS

challenges students to support that own views with evidence and argument. (Hare, 2009, p. 39)

It is, I think, no coincidence that some of the most concrete pedagogical strategies to arise from Hare's treatment of open-mindedness in education concern the fostering of inquiry, curiosity, wonder, and questioning. As Hare comments (2011): "A vital clue is found in Russell's fundamental insight that open-mindedness will always exist where desire for knowledge is genuine (Russell, 1973, p. 133)." What is good questioning if not a genuine desire for knowledge combined with the ability to seek it out. I conclude, then, by simply restating the central claim that open-mindedness can be exercised and cultivated in the form of good questioning.

Acknowledgments

This work was supported by a John Templeton Foundation grant (no. 61413). The views expressed are those of the author and do not reflect the views of the John Templeton Foundation.

Notes

1. https://narratively.com/i-escaped-the-cult-but-i-couldnt-escape-the-cult-mental ity/. Accessed February 28, 2022.
2. The parentheses here and in the title are used to indicate the scope and focus of the chapter rather than the relative significance of questioning versus listening with respect to open-mindedness. Indeed, I think it highly plausible that good questioning without good listening would often, if not typically, fall short of open-mindedness. As it happens, my interest and expertise lie in the domain of questioning, rather than listening, hence the scope and focus of this chapter on the former. However, I believe that a complete answer to the how-to challenge addressed here must also consider the significant role of listening in the cultivation and exercise of open-mindedness. For relevant work in this area, I refer the reader to Beatty 1999, Rice and Burbles 2010, Cohen 2014, and Notess 2019.
3. Note that I am *not* claiming that information-seeking is the only goal or function of questioning. We, of course, ask questions for many different reasons. I have argued elsewhere that information-seeking is nonetheless the *defining* function of questioning. As such, we can do a multitude of things with questions but questioning is still, in essence, an information-seeking act. I defend this view most extensively in Watson 2021a.
4. Naturally, there is more to be said about the precise nature of what I am calling "worthwhile information" here. In particular, one may ask whether a questioner's ability to seek worthwhile information ultimately relies on her ability to identify

HOW TO BE OPEN-MINDED 165

information that has some form of intrinsic or fundamental value. This question draws us toward the question of what makes any epistemic good valuable and, as such, extends far beyond the scope of this chapter. Here, as elsewhere, I believe I can tentatively sidestep this complex territory by noting that in order to get a functioning notion of good questioning off the ground, one must simply acknowledge that there is sometimes some information that is more worth having than other information, and that part of what it is to be a good questioner is to be able to target the former and avoid the latter. This of course leaves the account of good questioning underspecified in certain important respects but none of these affect the central claim or argument in this chapter. I touch on this point in several other places including Watson 2018, 2019, 2022b.

5. https://narratively.com/i-escaped-the-cult-but-i-couldnt-escape-the-cult-mentality/. Accessed February 28, 2022.
6. https://narratively.com/i-escaped-the-cult-but-i-couldnt-escape-the-cult-mentality/. Accessed February 28, 2022.
7. Condition (c) in the account is no less significant and, I think, speaks to the central import of good listening alongside good questioning, in the exercise of open-mindedness. As already noted, my focus is on questioning as opposed to listening so I will not consider condition (c) in this chapter. It is nonetheless worth noting that this condition is captured in several other prominent expositions of open-mindedness. Hare (2003), for example, places "critical receptiveness" at the heart of his account of open-mindedness (a notion that he borrows from Russell). Hare says, "Critical receptiveness involves a readiness to consider new ideas together with a commitment to accept only those that pass scrutiny" (p. 79). This notion of critical receptiveness again speaks to the central import of listening in the exercise of open-mindedness.
8. Of course, one can object to Baehr's characterization of the activity of transcending and its role in open-mindedness. It is therefore worth noting that nothing I have said about the conceptual overlap between open-mindedness and questioning ultimately relies on the tight conceptual connection between transcending and questioning that I have identified here. There are many other ways of illuminating the relationship between open-mindedness and questioning and I explore some of these in relation to different accounts of open-mindedness in the literature in due course.
9. As before, I note that we, of course, ask questions for many different reasons. As such, a recognition that we are missing some piece of information, etc., is not always what moves us to ask questions. I maintain, nonetheless, that questions are premised on this recognition, in the sense that, without it the practice of questioning, in general, would not exist. I defend this view most extensively in Watson 2022c. There is also a recent literature in epistemology, centrally featuring, e.g., Friedman (2017) and Whitcomb (2017), which defends a related "ignorance norm for inquiry."
10. https://narratively.com/i-escaped-the-cult-but-i-couldnt-escape-the-cult-mentality/. Accessed February 28, 2022.

Works Cited

Adler, Jonathan. 2004. "Reconciling Open-Mindedness and Belief." *Theory and Research in Education* 2(2): 127–142.

Baehr, Jason. 2011. "The Structure of Open-Mindedness." *Canadian Journal of Philosophy* 41(2): 191–213.

Battaly, Heather. 2004. Must the Intellectual Virtues Be Reliable? *Presented at 7th Annual Inland Northwest Philosophy Conference, 5/1/2004,* Washington State University.

166 THE VIRTUE OF OPEN-MINDEDNESS

Battaly, Heather. 2018. "Can Closed-Mindedness Be an Intellectual Virtue?" *Royal Institute of Philosophy Supplement* 84, 23–45.

Beatty, Joseph. 1999. "Good Listening." *Educational Theory* 49(3): 281–298.

Carter, J. Adam and Emma C. Gordon. 2014. "Openmindedness and Truth." *Canadian Journal of Philosophy* 44(2): 207–224.

Cohen, Jonathan, R. 2014. "Open-Minded Listening." *Charlotte Law Review* 5: 139–162.

Fantl, Jeremy. 2018. *The Limitations of the Open Mind*. Oxford: Oxford University Press.

Friedman, Jane. 2017. "Why Suspend Judging?" *Noûs* 51(2): 302–326.

Hare, William. 2003. "The Ideal of Open-Mindedness and Its Place in Education." *Journal of Thought* 38(2): 3–10.

Hare, William. 2009. "What Open-Mindedness Requires." *Skeptical Inquirer* 33(2): 36–39.

Hare, William. 2011. "Helping Open-Mindedness Flourish." *Journal of Thought* 46(1–2): 9–20.

Kwong, Jack, M. C. 2016. "Open-Mindedness as Engagement." *Southern Journal of Philosophy* 54(1): 70–86.

Notess, Susan. 2019. "Listening to People: Using Social Psychology to Spotlight an Overlooked Virtue." *Philosophy* 94(4): 621–643.

Rice, Suzanne and Nichalos C. Burbules. 2010. "Listening: A Virtue Account." *Teachers College Record* 112(11): 2728–2742.

Riggs, Wayne. 2010. "Open-Mindedness." *Metaphilosophy* 41(1-2): 172–188.

Rothstein, Dan and Luz Santana. 2011. *Make Just One Change: Teach Students to Ask Their Own Questions*. Cambridge, MA: Harvard Education Press.

Russel, Bertrand. 1973. *On Education*. London: Unwin Books.

Spiegel, James, S. 2012. "Open-Mindedness and Intellectual Humility." *Theory and Research in Education* 10(1): 27–38.

Watson, Lani. 2016. "Why Should We Educate for Inquisitiveness?" In *Intellectual Virtues and Education: Essays in Applied Virtue Epistemology*, ed. Jason Baehr (pp. 38–53). New York: Routledge.

Watson, Lani. 2018. "Educating for Good Questioning: A Tool for Intellectual Virtues Education." *Acta Analytica* 33(3): 353–370.

Watson, Lani. 2019. "Educating for Good Questioning as a Democratic Skill." In *The Routledge Handbook of Social Epistemology*, ed. Miranda Fricker, Peter J. Graham, David Henderson, and Nikolaj J. L. L. Pedersen (pp. 437–446). New York: Routledge.

Watson, Lani. 2020. "'Knowledge Is Power': Barriers to Intellectual Humility in the Classroom." In *The Routledge Handbook of the Philosophy of Humility*, ed. M. Alfano, M. Lynch, and A. Tanesini, A. (pp. 439–450). London: Routledge.

Watson, Lani. 2021a. "What Is a Question?" *Philosophy*, *RIP Supplement* 89: 273–297.

Watson, Lani. 2021b. *The Right to Know: Epistemic Rights and Why We Need Them*. London: Routledge.

Watson, Lani. 2022a. "The Role of Curiosity in Successful Collaboration." *Scientia et Fides* 10(2): 31–49.

Watson, Lani. 2022b. "Cultivating Curiosity in the Information Age." *Philosophy*, *RIP Supplements* 92: 129–148.

HOW TO BE OPEN-MINDED 167

Watson, Lani. 2022c. "The Social Virtue of Questioning." In *Social Virtue Epistemology*, ed. M. Alfano, J. de Ridder, and C. Klein (pp. 424–441). New York: Routledge.

Whitcomb, Dennis. 2017. "One Kind of Asking." *Philosophical Quarterly* 67(266).

Zagzebski, Linda. 1996. *Virtues of the Mind: An Inquiry into the Nature of Virtue and the Ethical Foundations of Knowledge.* Cambridge: Cambridge University Press.

Index

For the benefit of digital users, indexed terms that span two pages (e.g., 52–53) may, on occasion, appear on only one of those pages.

Figures are indicated by an italic *f* following the page number.

Adler, Jonathan, 153, 154–55, 156, 157–58, 159
alternative facts, 106–7
amelioration, 49–51
American Civil Liberties Union, 112–13
animal suffering, 68–69, 74–75
Aristotle, 3, 102, 123, 124–25, 129, 134–35n.4
Asanga, 59–60
atomism, 4–5
attention, 23–26, 37

Bad Hand, Howard, 13, 16–17, 82–84, 85, 86–99
Baehr, Jason, 10–11, 15–16, 58, 59, 60–61, 86, 101–2, 105, 106, 131, 142–43, 147, 148–50, 151–52, 153, 155, 156, 165n.8
Basso, Keith, 84–85
Begby, Endre, 33–34
Berg, David, 140–41
Bing, Suzanne, 123–24, 129–30
Buddhism, 12–13, 16–17
  Abhidharma tradition, 12–13, 59–60, 62–63, 65
  on OM, 58–59, 72–73, 76
  perspective-taking in, 68–73, 74–75
  pliancy in, 59–68, 76

Camp, Elizabeth, 12, 16–17
Carnap, Rudolf, 33
Carter, J. Adam, 141–42
Cartesianism, 3
centrality, connection and, 26–27
ceremony, 87–91, 93–98
change, conservation and, 87–91
characterizational confirmation, 33–37

characterizations, 22–23, 29, 30–37, 47–48
checking, 154–55, 157, 159
Children of God (COG), 139, 140–41, 146–47, 154, 159–60, 161, 163
Chrisman, Matt, 2–3
climate change and global warming, 103, 105–6, 109, 149–50, 151, 159–60
closed-mindedness, 85, 89, 102, 106, 113–14, 115–16, 142–43, 146–47, 160
cognitive standpoint, OM and, 10–11, 102, 142
  default, transcending, 15–16, 58, 67, 68–73, 86, 101–2, 131, 142, 147, 148–49, 150, 151–52, 155, 156, 162–63
colonization and colonizers, 16, 79–81
Commedia dell' Arte, 126–27, 130
competency conditions, of good questioning, 143–44, 145, 157, 158–60
complacency, 38, 40, 47
connection, centrality and, 26–27
conservation, change and, 87–91
conspiracy theories, 44
Copeau, Jacques
  on masks, 16–17, 122–23, 124, 127–31, 137nn.33–34
  Montessori and, 14, 123–28, 129, 130, 131–34, 134n.1, 134–35n.4, 138n.48
  on open-mindedness in theater, 14–15, 16–17, 122–23, 125, 133–34
Currie, Gregory, 42

Dasté, Jean, 129, 137nn.33–34
Dei, George J. Sefa, 80–81

170 INDEX

Deloria, Vine, Jr., 81–82
democracy, 101, 105, 112, 116
Denma Lochö Rinpoche, 60
Descartes, René, 3–5, 6
diagnosticity, 24–26, 33–34
dualism, 6

embodiment, OM and, 64–66, 95–98
epistemic criterion, 103–4, 105
epistemic humility, 46–47, 122–23, 124,
131–32, 133–34, 138n.48
epistemic love, 124–25, 131, 133–34
epistemic virtue, OM as, 1, 3, 13, 59,
62–63, 67
epistemology
of Descartes, 3–5
HEP and, 3–8, 9–11
naturalism in, 2–4, 8
virtue, 131–34, 141–42, 148
evaluation, 27–29
exchanging self and other, 58, 70, 71,
72–73, 75–76
explanation, 37–38

fake news, 106–7, 113
fallibility, 153, 154–55, 156, 162–63
Fernbach, Philip, 8
FIRE. See Foundation for Individual
Rights in Education
First Amendment, 110–11
Foundation for Individual Rights in
Education (FIRE), 108
frames, 23, 33–34, 40, 41, 51
Frayn, Michael, 102
free speech, 101, 107–16
Friedman, Marilyn, 73
Frierson, Patrick, 131–32

Garvey, Peggy, 14–15, 16–17
Gestalt, 31, 38–39, 43–44
Goldman, Alvin, 42
Gone with the Wind (Mitchell), 22
good questioning, 15–16, 140–46, 147–
52, 157–60, 162–63, 164–65n.4, 164
Gordon, Emma C., 141–42
Grosfoguel, Ramón, 79–80

Hare, William, 86, 101–2, 104–5, 106,
110, 157–58, 163–64, 165n.7

Harold of Orange, 81–82
hate speech, 108–16
HEP. See Human Epistemic Predicament
hermeneutic impasses, 39, 41–42, 45–
47, 49
higher education and campus speech, 13–
14, 107–8, 110, 111–13, 114–16
Hill, William Ely, 32f
himpathy, 73–74
Human Epistemic Predicament (HEP),
3–8, 9–11
Hume, David, 46
Hyman, Wendy, 107–8

imagination, 41, 50
individualism, 4–5, 98–99
intellectual virtue, OM as, 102, 140, 141–
42, 148
intensity, in prominence, 24–26

Jackson, Rachael, 98–99
Jefferson, Thomas, 112–13

Kuhn, Thomas, 38–39
Kwong, Jack, 156

Lambie, John, 117n.16
liberal education, 42, 45
Lodrö, Geshe, 62

Maibom, Heidi, 75–76
Manne, Kate, 73–74
Marshall, Thurgood, 110–11
masks, 16–17, 122–23, 124, 127–31,
137nn.33–34
McRae, Emily, 12–13, 16–17
memory, 91–92
Mercier, Hugo, 6–8
#metoo movement, 73–74
mind-body dualism, 6
mindfulness, 128, 136n.26
Mipham Rinpoche, 61–62
Mitchell, Margaret, 22
Montessori, Maria, and Montessorian
educational methods, 14–15, 123–
28, 129, 130, 131–34, 134n.1, 134–
35n.4, 137n.28, 138n.48
Murray, Charles, 110, 114–16
myopia, 38, 40, 47, 49–50

INDEX 171

Narvaez, Darcia, 136n.26
Native Americans
  ceremony, 87–91, 93–98
  colonization, settler colonialism and,
    16, 79–81, 85–86, 98–99
  embodiment and, 95–98
  genocide of, 79–80, 83, 85–86
  perspective on OM, 13, 79–80, 81–99
  relationships and, 93–95
  transpersonal experience and, 91–93
  trickster analytic approach, 81–87
naturalism, in epistemology, 2–4, 8
Nehamas, Alexander, 44, 50
Nietzsche, Friedrich, 123, 124, 127–29
normativity and normative theories,
  2–3, 11

Obama, Barack, 112–13
OM. *See* open-mindedness
open-mindedness (OM)
  affective dimensions of, 66–68
  Baehr on, 10–11, 15–16, 58, 59, 60–61,
    86, 101–2, 105, 106, 131, 142–43,
    147, 148–50, 151–52, 153, 155,
    156, 165n.8
  Buddhism on, 58–59, 72–73, 76
  ceremony and, 87–91, 93–98
  cognitive standpoint and, 10–11,
    15–16, 58, 67, 86, 101–2, 131, 142,
    147, 148–49, 150, 151–52, 155,
    156, 162–63
  controversial issues and, 103–4, 105–
    7, 113–14
  Copeau on, 14–15, 16–17, 122–23,
    125, 133–34
  critical, 117n.16
  cultivating, 139–40, 160–64
  embodiment and, 64–66, 95–98
  epistemic humility and, 131–32
  as epistemic virtue, 1, 3, 13, 59, 62–
    63, 67
  exercising, 139–40, 145–60
  free speech, hate speech and, 110–16
  free speech and, 101, 107–8
  good questioning and, 15–16, 140–46,
    147–52, 157–60, 162–63, 164
  Hare on, 86, 101–2, 104–5, 106, 110,
    157–58, 163–64, 165n.7
  HEP and, 9–11

  as intellectual virtue, 102, 140, 141–
    42, 148
  memory and, 91–92
  mental flexibility in, 72
  moral dimensions of, 61–63
  Native American perspective on, 13,
    79–80, 81–99
  perspectival, 39–42, 45
  pliancy and, 59–68, 76
  questioning and, 152–56
  relationships and, 93–95
  Riggs on, 86, 101–3, 141–42, 153, 154,
    155–56, 157–58, 162
  right *versus* left, 104–10
  teachers promoting and cultivating,
    102–3, 105–7, 162–64
  transpersonal experience and, 91–93
  trickster analytic approach to, 81–87
Owens, Justine E., 66

Palfrey, John, 115
Patrul Rinpoche, 68–70, 74
perspectival complacency, 33–39, 49–50
perspectival OM, 39–42, 45
perspectival perpetuation, 37–39
perspectival perversion, 42–45, 49–50
perspectival play, 41, 50
perspectival variation, 20–21, 22
perspectives
  amelioration and, 49–51
  aptness of, 45–49
  attention, prominence and, 23–26
  characterizations and, 22–23, 29, 30–
    37, 47–48
  cognitive standpoints and, 101–2
  connection, centrality and, 26–27
  as double-edged swords, 19–20, 33
  in fiction, 22, 41–42
  flexible, 19–20, 29–30, 33, 38, 41, 50
  frames and, 23, 33–34, 40, 41, 51
  hermeneutic impasses and, 39, 41–42,
    45–47, 49
  political, religious, and scientific, 20–22
  predication, evaluation, response and,
    27–29
  propositions and, 29–33
  stereotypes, characterizational
    confirmation and, 33–37
  touchstone cases of, 20–23

172 INDEX

perspective-taking, 68–76
physical theater, 122–23, 124–25
Plato, 45–46
pliancy
  affective dimensions of, 66–69
  moral dimensions of, 61–63, 68–69
  OM and, 59–68, 76
  physical dimensions of, 64–66, 68–69
prediction, evaluation, and response,
  27–29
prominence, attention and, 23–26

Question Formulation Technique, 162
questioning, 152–56. *See also* good
  questioning

racism and racist speech, 110, 113–16
Randall, Alice, 22
Réflexions sur le Paradox de Diderot
  (Copeau), 130
relationships, OM and, 93–95
relativism, 46, 49
response, 27–29
Riggs, Wayne, 86, 101–3, 141–42, 153,
  154, 155–56, 157–58, 162
Robbins, Rockey, 13, 16–17
Robertson, Emily, 13–14, 16, 17
Ross, Loretta J., 116

Saint-Denis, Michel, 134n.1, 137n.33
Śāntideva, 69–73, 74, 75–76
self-centered standpoint, 69–70, 72, 76
settler colonialism, 79–81, 85–86,
  98–99
Sloman, Steven, 8
Sperber, Dan, 6–8

stereotypes, 33–37
Sun Dance ceremony, 87, 88, 89–
  90, 93–98

taxonomy, 24, 26, 29, 37
Taylor, Rebecca, 114
Toth, Christie, 98–99
transpersonal experience, 91–93
trickster analytic, 81–87
Trump, Donald, 63, 107–8, 110
Tversky, Amos, 24

Vasubandhu, 60, 64–66
Vieux Colombier, Le, 123–24, 137n.33
virtue
  Aristotle on, 3, 102
  epistemic, 1, 3, 13, 59, 62–63, 67
  intellectual, 102, 140, 141–42, 148
  of pliancy, 61–63
virtue epistemology, 131–34, 141–42, 148
Vizenor, Gerald, 81–82, 84, 98–99

Waldron, Jeremy, 108–10
Watson, Lani, 15–16, 17
whiteness, 84–85
Wiles, David, 129
Wind Done Gone, The (Randall), 22
worthwhile information-seeking, in good
  questioning, 144–45, 157, 158–60,
  164–65n.4

Yiannopoulos, Milo, 107–8, 113
Young, Daniella, 15, 139–41, 146–47, 154,
  159–60, 161, 163

Zagzebski, Linda, 148